MGB and MGC

JONATHAN EDWARDS

The Crowood Press

First published in 2001 by
The Crowood Press Ltd
Ramsbury, Marlborough
Wiltshire SN8 2HR

British Library Cataloguing-in-Publication Data
A catalogue record for this book is available from the British Library.

ISBN 1 86126 469 0

Typeset and designed by Shane O'Dwyer, 18 Theobald Street, Swindon

Printed and bound in Singapore by Craft Print International Ltd.

CONTENTS

MGB: Family Life   4

1   Introduction   5

2   MGB   Mk I – 1962 to 1967   11

3   MGB Mk II – 1967 to 1974   27

4   MGB Mk II Black-Bumper model – 1974 to 1980   45

5   MGC – 1967 to 1969   59

6   MGB GT V8 – 1973 to 1976   73

Epilogue   89

Index   96

MGB: FAMILY LIFE

1958	Project work on MGB began
1960	Basic engineering design completed
20 September 1962	Introduction of MGB, with four-cylinder 1,798cc engine
January 1963	Laycock overdrive became an option
October 1964	Five-main-bearing engine replaced original three-main-bearing type
October 1965	Introduction of MGB GT, with Salisbury-type rear axle
April 1967	Salisbury rear axle standardized, all types
October 1967	Introduction of MGC (Roadster or GT Coupe), with six-cylinder 2,912cc engine and torsion bar front suspension MGB Mk II replaced MGB Mk I, with all-synchromesh gearbox, or Borg Warner automatic transmission option
October 1968	Revised gearbox and axle ratios for MGC models
September 1969	MGC models discontinued
October 1969	Improvements for 1970 Model Year, including recessed grille
September 1970	Improvements for 1971 Model Year
October 1971	Improvements for 1972 Model Year
October 1972	Improvements for 1973 Model Year, including reversion to traditional grille
August 1973	Introduction of MGB GT V8, with V8-cylinder 3,528cc engine
September 1973	Automatic transmission option discontinued
September 1974	New style for 1975 Model Year, including black polyurethane bumpers and increased ride height
May 1975	Anniversary (MG fiftieth) GT model built, 750-off
June 1975	Overdrive standardized
August 1976	Improvements for 1977 Model Year, including revised suspension package and new facia style
September 1976	MGB GT V8 model discontinued
October 1980	Production of final LE (Limited Edition) series of Roadster and GT models
23 October 1980	Classic MGB model finally discontinued
October 1992	RV8 Roadster model introduced, with V8 3,946cc engine and five-speed manual transmission
22 November 1995	RV8 Roadster discontinued

CHAPTER ONE

Introduction

BY the 1950s, MG had become the car company by which any other maker of sports cars measured itself. Any potential rival realized that it would be difficult to match the image that MG had built up – an image that combined style, performance and motor sport success with expertise in building two-seaters at an attractive price. Several tried, but very few even came close to shaping up.

MG, after all, had already been doing a superb job for more than thirty years, and knew exactly how to satisfy its clientele. In the late 1950s, it was building MGAs in big numbers and its factory was also being used for the assembly of Austin-Healey sports cars – and the company was ambitious to go one stage better for the 1960s.

The result of a lot of planning, made public in 1962, was the MGB. It was a sports car that was intended to go faster, to sell faster and to make more money, over a longer period, than any previous MG. Even so, before it was put on sale, no one could have forecast that it would stay in production for eighteen years, or that more than half-a-million examples would be built.

The MGB, in other words, would not only set new MG standards, but it would also set new world sports car standards. Not until some years after its demise would any other sports car sell in higher numbers. Popular then, it is legendary today, the archetypal 'classic car' by which all other machines are measured.

FINE HERITAGE

MG was not, and never has been, an independent concern. Founded in the 1920s, it was originally controlled by William Morris (who became Lord

The classic nose of the MGB first appeared in 1962. More than half-a-million such sports cars were built in the next eighteen years.

Striking and individual in 1962, the profile of the MGB never dated – and is quite unmistakable even today.

Nuffield in the 1930s). From 1935 it became a more closely integrated part of the Nuffield Organisation, and once Nuffield merged in 1952 with its deadly rivals, Austin, MG automatically became part of BMC, the British Motor Corporation.

Since 1929, however, MG sports cars had been built in a small, simply equipped but dedicated factory at Abingdon, just a few miles south of Oxford. In many ways, this meant that it could remain, and feel, isolated, ignoring the commercial and financial shenanigans that sometimes raged around it.

There had been several important 'landmark' events since then. The first purpose-built MG sports car to have its own chassis had been the 18/80 of 1928, the world-famous Midget line had been established at the same time, and a production rate of more than fifty cars a week had been superseded for the first time in 1937.

Post-war expansion had been rapid and impressive. Exports to North America began in 1947, the first independently suspended road car (the TD) was sold in 1950, and the first two-seater with all-enveloping coachwork, the MGA, followed in 1955. With MG's first unit-construction sports car – the Sprite-derived Midget – due to be launched in 1961, technical and marketing progress had been steady for some time.

OPPORTUNITIES

Throughout this period, MG was delighted to note that there seemed to be no limit to the demand for its cars, and any new model would have to take account of that. Each previous model had outsold the last, so there was every hope that the new car would carry on that trend.

Look at the figures – in the 1930s 2,083 J2 Midgets had been succeeded by 2,526 PA/PB types,

and then by 3,382 TA/TB types. After World War Two there had been 10,000 TCs, and every indication that more than 100,000 MGAs would be produced before the MGB took over. In modern times, the major difference was MG could only make one sports model, which therefore had to appeal to a wide market.

Abingdon's engineers already knew that any such new model would have to be produced with the minimum of newly designed chassis components. Purists might complain that MG sports cars did not contain unique engines, transmissions or suspensions, but most of them also understood the corporate reasoning behind it all. It was a matter of pure economics, for even in the 1950s no subsidiary company making less than 20,000 cars a year could possibly finance unique running gear.

There were MG precedents for this. The M-Type Midget of 1928, after all, had been based on the Morris Minor saloon, the T-Series Midgets had used many Nuffield components from Morris and Wolseley saloons, and the MGA, from stem to stern, used mainly modified BMC B-Series running gear. It followed that a successor would have to do the same.

Naturally, the shape, form and layout of the MGB were developed after a close study of the current marketplace – particularly that of North America, where the majority of all sports cars were being sold – and by learning from the experience built up with the MGA.

The MGA, in fact, had been a pivotal model for MG, so a very brief summary of its history is worthwhile. By the early 1950s its predecessors, the T-Series sports cars, had come to look old-fashioned, so a dramatic new look was essential. On the other hand, BMC corporate policy meant that the MGA would have to be designed around corporate (though modern) BMC saloon car running gear.

Accordingly, for the MGA, management was allowed to design a completely new chassis and a new (and visually very attractive) body style. For all the usual investment reasons, this meant that the new model would have to 'pay for itself' by selling in large numbers, and remaining on sale for more than five years – and in the end that 'life' would be stretched most successfully to seven years.

Although the front suspension and rack and pinion steering were lifted virtually unchanged from the previous model (the TF), the pushrod overhead-valve engine, the four-speed gearbox and the hypoid bevel rear axle were all developed versions of the new BMC B-Series range which was already being used in cars as various as the MG Magnette ZA saloon, the Austin Cambridge saloon – as well as a variety of light commercial vehicles!

MGB AND THE MARKETPLACE

A successor to the MGA would have to face a marketplace which, in the 1960s, was already well-stocked with rivals. Whereas the MGA had only had to face up to the Triumph TR2, the starting grid was to be more crowded this time around.

Not only would there be a new-generation Triumph TR (the TR4 was introduced in 1961), but there was also the Sunbeam Alpine, along with growing competition from Fiat's 1500 Cabriolet. However, while Alfa Romeo Giulietta Spiders were faster, and very pretty, they cost a lot more money, while 'in-house' competition from the Austin-Healey 3000 did not really count as

this big, hairy-chested machine was fitted with a 2.9-litre six-cylinder engine.

At this stage in motoring history, there was no competition from Japan, although this would not last for long. The promising 1.5-litre Nissan/Datsun Fairlady would appear in 1962, to be succeeded by the SP311 model (which drew on the MGB as its inspiration) in 1965.

By the end of the 1950s, of the 15,000–20,000 cars which were being built every year, the vast majority of MGAs were being exported. Statistics show that only 5.5 per cent of them were originally delivered to British market customers. As the North American market was becoming commercially more important with every year that passed, any new MG model would have to take account of that.

First thoughts on a new car – coded EX214 in the MG list of projects – took shape in 1958, and though the designers dearly wanted to make a real technological leap forward, almost immediately a number of the designers' ambitious ideas had to be modified. MG's general manager, John Thornley, knew that the existing MGA was too heavy and had a slightly cramped cabin, with both of these factors being influenced by the use of a separate chassis.

Naturally, he wanted to see the new car improve on this, by using a unit-construction body/chassis (which one of BMC's favoured suppliers, Pressed Steel Co. Ltd, would provide), but for a time it looked as if high investment/tooling costs might kill off that plan. In the end, Thornley

Styled in 1960, the MGB always looked good from every angle. This was the original version, this car dating from 1964.

broke the impasse by squeezing down the capital costs but agreeing to pay £2 extra for every shell actually delivered to Abingdon.

At Abingdon, this was not the first monocoque car with which the design staff had been involved, for the Magnette saloon and the Austin-Healey Frogeye Sprite (neither of which they had designed) were already well known. Moreover, work on an MG Midget derivative of the restyled Sprite was already going ahead.

By choosing a monocoque for the new car, this allowed the cockpit to be repackaged and, as a direct consequence, the wheelbase to be shortened. Originally, it had been hoped to use independent rear suspension, but no suitable chassis-mounted final-drive ratio was available. Next, a coil spring/radius arm/Panhard rod location of the B-Series axle was developed, the first prototype actually having that layout. Finally, however, testing experience caused this to be rejected, and a change was made to a conventional half-elliptic leaf-spring location. This, incidentally, meant that the rear of the car had to be slightly lengthened to accommodate the underbody changes that followed.

By 1960–61, therefore, the layout of the MGB which we all know had been finalized. Not only did it use the same basic front suspension layout as the MGA, but it also used an uprated version of the MGA 1600 Mk II's power train, the difference being that the engine capacity was pushed out from 1,622cc to 1,798cc, which was almost its practical limit.

In the beginning, this engine still had a three-bearing crankshaft, although a five-bearing version was known to be under development. The gearbox still did not have synchromesh on first gear, and – as was normal with an MG – there was no overdrive option at first, although once again this fitting was also under development.

Compared with the MGA, the MGB also had much smoother lines and a more roomy cockpit, plus wind-up windows. All this, combined with the 'Abingdon touch', made this a good basis for a new line of MG sports cars.

PRODUCTION				CALENDAR YEAR	
YEAR	MGB ROADSTER	MGB GT	MGC ROADSTER	MGC GT	MG MGB V8
1962	4,518	–	–	–	–
1963	23,308	–	–	–	–
1964	26,542	–	–	–	–
1965	24,179	–	–	524	–
1966	22,675	10,241	9	4	–
1967	15,128	11,396	182	38	–
1968	17,355	8,352	2,596	2,491	–
1969	18,887	12,135	1,757	1,925	–
1970	23,662	12,510	–	–	–
1971	22,511	12,169	–	–	–
1972	26,222	13,171	–	–	3
1973	19,546	10,208	–	–	1,070
1974	19,757	9,626	–	–	853
1975	20,171	4,517	–	–	482
1976	25,527	3,656	–	–	183
1977	24,483	4,198	–	–	–
1978	21,702	5,652	–	–	–
1979	19,897	3,503	–	–	–
1980	10,891	3,424	–	–	–
TOTALS	386,961	125,282	4,544	4,458	2,591

In addition, 2,000 MG RV8s were built from 1993 to 1995.

The original MGB featured this 95bhp B-series engine. Over the years the fittings, pipework and anti-emissions gear would proliferate, but the basic unit would be unchanged.

BELOW: With assistance from Pininfarina, MG developed the ultra-smart MGB GT, which sold in large quantities from 1965 to 1980.

BOTTOM: MGBs became Mk IIs from 1967, and were facelifted again for the 1970s. This GT dates from 1973.

ABOVE: The first major evolution of the MGB design came in 1967, with the launch of the six-cylinder engined MGC.

LEFT: When the MGB GT V8 was announced in 1973, it was the fastest MG of all time.

BELOW: For the MGB the end of the line came in 1980, when a final batch of UK-market Limited-Edition models were built.

CHAPTER TWO

MGB Mk I

BECAUSE the MGA had always sold so well, and because the MG factory at Abingdon was in any case well-occupied with the build-up of Midget assembly *and* the introduction of a new derivative of the Austin-Healey 3000, there was no unseemly rush to bring the new MGB to market. However, it was always the plan to start building a few cars before high summer, to begin volume assembly in the autumn and have the 'pipeline' to North America well filled before the start of a new calendar year.

On that basis, therefore, the introduction of the MGB was even more briskly effected than usual. The very first MGB production car (chassis number 101) took shape in May 1962, MGA assembly closed down in July, and MGB series production was already established by the holiday 'shut-down' in July/August 1962. Despite this, the car was not launched to the public until September 1962. It was such a smooth process that no fewer than 4,518 of the new soft-top cars – always known (but not badged) as the Roadster – had been produced by the end of the calendar year.

Originally announced in 1962. the MGB Roadster looked like this for the next three years. The colour is British Racing Green, and of course, the club badge is an extra fitting. Until 1966, front overriders were optional extras on Home Market cars.

It should be acknowledged, however, that this achievement had not been easy. First and foremost was the fact that the MGB's structure was totally new, and although broadly similar running gear to the MGA was to be employed, the whole would have to go together in a way which was fresh for Abingdon.

The MGB had a monocoque (unit-construction) structure, whereas the MGA had used a separate chassis. The MGB had a 1.8-litre, not a 1.6-litre, engine. The assembly process at Abingdon had to be altered to make provision for a monocoque painted/trimmed body shell to arrive from Morris Bodies Branch, with engines and suspensions being offered up in a different sequence. Preparations (though not for immediate use) would also have to be made for offering up long and bulky engine/gearbox *and* overdrive assemblies, and an alternative body style. And more, and more …

There was never any shortage of demand, however, and Abingdon's workforce did its usual remarkable job in shaking down a new car – after the first 4,518 MGBs were produced in 1962, another 23,308 would follow in 1963. That figure, on its own, was already better than had ever been achieved with the MGA. Onwards and upwards, it seemed …

As originally planned, the MGB might only have had a seven-year career, and might have been totally replaced by about 1969–70, but things did not quite work out like that. First of all, the original type of MGB, would be built for five seasons, before being substantially revised. At the same time, a new derivative – the six-cylinder-engined MGC – would arrive on the scene, and shortly after that MG would find itself part of the giant new British Leyland combine.

In retrospect, the first five years were a happy time for the MGB, as few enforced changes had to be made; it was still possible to export cars to North America with substantially the same specification as that of UK-market cars. All that would change – dramatically in some cases – after 1968.

In the first five years, though, not only would a different type of 1.8-litre engine be specified from late 1964, but overdrive would become available for the very first time on any MG, and an extremely smart MGB GT coupe/hatchback would join the family from late 1965. This original-type MGB was only discontinued because the Mk II that followed it was a substantially better car.

STRUCTURE

Like the MG Midget that had preceded it at Abingdon, the MGB had a sturdy monocoque bodyshell, where there was no separate chassis. The structure was made entirely out of sheet steel, with what looked like 'chassis legs' running back on each side of the engine bay to a cross-member behind the line of the gearbox. Much rigidity was built in by the transmission tunnel, and by using double-section sills under the doors. Other stiffening came from the rigid bulkhead separating the engine bay from the passenger compartment, and from the pressed steel inner wheel arches.

The front suspension was carried on a separate steel cross member bolted up to the structure and the front wings were bolt-on steel pressings (the rear wings were welded in place). The bonnet pressing was the only panel on this car to be manufactured in aluminium; *all* other panels were in steel. As on the MGA, and on the smaller Midget, the windscreen surround was bolted into place, rather than being welded into the structure when it was manufactured.

From late 1965 the GT version of the bodyshell was added to the range, the structure being changed to include permanently welded windscreen pillars (and a deeper windscreen), a roof panel and an upward-opening hatchback. Changes were also made around the rear floor area, to allow a small (and practically useless) fold-down 'occasional' rear seat to be fitted above the rear axle line.

RUNNING GEAR

The engine, gearbox and rear axle on the original MGBs were all developed B-Series versions of those found in the previous MGA type.

In the case of the MGB, the 18G-type engine was a 95bhp/1,798cc derivative (no other BMC car ever had this type of engine fitted), with three crankshaft main bearings, along with twin semi-downdraught SU carburettors and twin exhaust downpipes from a new cast manifold. The only important change came in February 1964, when closed-circuit crankcase breathing was adopted.

From October 1964, the 18GA-type of engine took over, which was rated the same, and looked the same from outside, but had five crankshaft main bearings, and therefore a new and more rigid crank. In a whole variety of tunes, this five-bearing unit was subsequently adopted on many other BMC cars and light commercial vehicles.

The four-speed gearbox was basically a standard BMC B-Series assembly, with no synchromesh on first gear, but with a unique gear-change layout. A closer-ratio gear set was also available as a motorsport accessory.

From early 1963 (after less than 10,000 cars had been built) a Laycock D-type overdrive, with a step-up ratio of 0.802:1, became an option. This operated, by way of a facia-mounted switch, on top and third gears only.

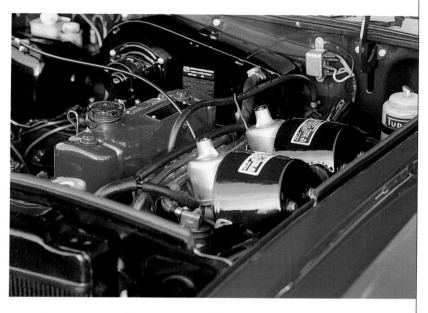

Compared with the MGA, there was more space around the engine of the MGB, though this was still quite a bonnet-full of machinery. Twin SU HS4 carburettors and Cooper air filters were standard equipment.

Original cars used a 'banjo'-type of B-Series hypoid rear axle, which tended to be noisy – this was never used on GT models. When that derivative was introduced, this model was given a sturdier and more refined Salisbury-type of axle (with the same 3.909:1 ratio), assembled and housed in a different manner, and tending to be quieter and more refined. The Salisbury axle was also standardized on Roadsters from spring 1967, the process being complete by July 1967.

SUSPENSION, STEERING AND BRAKES

Independent front suspension was by a modified MGA-type of coil spring/wishbone layout, where the lever arms for the hydraulic shock absorbers also doubled as 'top wishbones'. There was no anti-roll bar in the standard specification, though one was always available as an optional extra (it was standardized from November 1966). When the GT version arrived, an anti-roll bar was standard on that version of the car, while GT spring rates were always slightly different from those of the Roadster.

Rack and pinion steering was fitted, naturally without power-assistance. Depending on the territory to be served, cars were equipped with steering column lock/ignition keys. The steering wheel featured wire-spokes in a T-formation.

Front suspension and steering were all carried on the pressed steel front cross member, which was bolted up under the monocoque. The rear suspension was simplicity itself – the axle was located and sprung on long, half-elliptic, multi-leaf springs, controlled by lever-arm hydraulic dampers. There were no extra radius arms or Panhard rods of any type, nor an anti-roll bar. Because

of their extra weight, GT models had firmer springs than the Roadsters.

All cars were fitted with a Lockheed disc front/drum rear braking installation – there was no servo, even as an option (this would not arrive until 1970, on the next model).

The original MGB was always available with a choice of 14in perforated disc, or painted centre-lock, wire-spoke wheels, and tyres were 5.60-14 cross-plys. At this time, radial-ply tyres were not available, not even as options.

ELECTRICAL EQUIPMENT

Like all other BMC cars of the period, the MGB had stem to stern Lucas electrical components. Positive earth circuitry was still employed, there was an M418G inertia-type starter motor, and the direct current generator was a C40-1 dynamo.

Power was supplied by two Lucas 6-volt batteries, connected 'in-line' – these being positioned in cradles, low down, on either side of the propeller shaft line, under removable panels in the tonneau area behind the seats.

COCKPIT AND TRIM

Not only did the MGB have a more spacious cabin than the MGA had done (in spite of its shorter wheelbase, the packaging had been improved), but the standard of trim and equipment was also an advance. A major innovation, made necessary in order for the MGB to keep up with its competitors, was to use wind-up windows, with small swivelling quarter windows at the front of those windows as well.

Original Roadsters were equipped with a 'pack away' (or 'build-it-yourself') set of soft-top frame tubes, over which the plastic soft-top had to be draped and fastened or – as an optional extra – a permanently attached folding hood/soft-top was also available. Many cars were also sold with a separate tonneau cover. On the MGB GT, the lift-up hatchback/loading door consisted almost entirely of glass.

The original interior trim was characterized by leather facings with colour-contrast piping on the seats, the door trim panels being neatly styled to match. There was wall-to-wall carpet, under and behind the seats too. On the Roadster, a rear seat cushion was an option, but since rear leg room was non-existent this was only of marginal function.

The GT's layout was similar, except that a tiny, fold-flat rear 'occasional' seat was included, which was useful for carrying shopping or carrycots, but little more. The GT's loading area was neatly carpeted, although the interior of the Roadster's boot compartment was bare of trim.

A lift-off hardtop, smart, with a large rear window, and with extra quarter windows behind the doors, became optional in June 1963.

The facia was simply laid out and well-equipped, with the rev counter and speedometer ahead of the driver's eyes. The panel itself was black-crackle painted metal, and although there was provision for a radio and a heater, neither was standard (although because these items were optional, many cars had them fitted when new, or shortly afterwards).

Safety-belt mountings were standard, but the belts themselves remained as a dealer-fitted accessory option until April 1967, belts were then fitted as standard thereafter. Few customers bothered with them at first – the atmosphere towards safety was somewhat different in those days!

PRODUCTION

By the 1960s, MG's Abingdon factory was only an assembly plant, not a manufacturing operation, with virtually every component of the cars – structures, drive train and other major components – being manufactured elsewhere. MGB manufacture, therefore, depended on regular supplies from other factories, all of which were brought in by truck; their delivery to the factory was consequently dependent on the weather and road conditions. In blizzard conditions, new supplies soon ran out, and MGB production ground to a halt!

For this model (although things would change in the late 1960s), all Roadster major body pressings were stamped out by Pressed Steel at Swindon. They were then sent to the Morris Bodies Branch in Coventry for jigging and welding into monocoques, which were then painted and trimmed, before being trucked back down to Abingdon, six at a time.

MGB GT shells, on the other hand, were always completely pressed and assembled at Swindon, trucked to Cowley (the 'Morris Motors' factory) for paint and trim, and then trucked to Abingdon. This explains, incidentally, why the colour range for Roadsters was different from that of the GT, for two different paint shops were involved – Abingdon never had its own paint facility.

1.8-litre B-Series engines were manufactured at the 'Austin' factory at Longbridge (among every other derivative of this versatile BMC 'building block'), while transmissions were manufactured close by and were then mated to the engines at Longbridge, the whole then being delivered to Abingdon.

There were two types of rear axle – the original Roadsters had a corporate B-Series unit made at BMC's 'Tractors and Transmissions' factory in Birmingham (this factory had once built Wolseley cars), but the GT (and, from 1967, the Roadster)

This is the facia/instrument display of an MGB Mk I, this car dating from 1964. The radio fitted to this car was an accessory, although provision was always made in the facia style for it to be added. Safety belts were also an accessory – the reinforced mountings already being in place.

DATES	May 1962–October 1967
CHASSIS NUMBERS	101–138799 (Roadster)
	71933–139823 (GT)
PRODUCTION BREAK POINTS	five-bearing engine from 48766
TOTAL PRODUCED	115,898 Roadster
	21,835 GT

Until 1965, door handles were of the simple pull-out variety, like this, but were then replaced by the fix-handle/push-button type which looked almost the same.

had a different Salisbury design of axle, made by the same subsidiary.

Front suspension pieces, the steering rack, brakes (originally from Lockheed in Leamington Spa), electrical kits from Lucas in the Birmingham area, instruments from Smiths Industries, and trim items from all over the industry, all flooded into Abingdon by transporter. Virtually nothing was actually manufactured at the simply equipped Abingdon plant itself.

Bodyshells met their running gear at Abingdon by being lowered carefully on to cradles carrying them at the upper level of the tracks (on the 'trim decks'), and much of the labour was concerned with kitting out the almost-equipped cars after that.

At a certain point, the nearly complete shells were lowered on to the 'Elevated Lines' for all underside work to be carried out, then lowered to ground level for completion. From the start there were three parallel lines, all pumping out MGBs, and when the Austin-Healey 3000 model closed down the MGB took up that space too!

In spite of the high rate of production, however, Abingdon did not have powered, 'pull-along' assembly lines, so the cars were always pushed along on trolleys, then set up on their wheels as soon as possible, so that they could be pushed, by muscle power, from one station to the next.

CAREER

Once established, the original MGB enjoyed a very stable life, as neither the basic style, nor the technical specification, needed to change dramatically. Except in important detail and in the way that certain options had been standardized, a mid-1967 MGB Tourer was much like the late-1962 car that had started it all.

Throughout the five years, there would be no basic change to the 95bhp/1.8-litre/four-speed gearbox spec, and none at all to the car's shape, though a folding hood/soft-top was standardized from August 1963. However, from late 1964 the engine was equipped with a five-bearing crankshaft, and from early 1963 a Laycock overdrive became an optional extra. Standardization of the front anti-roll bar came in November 1966, with the heavier Salisbury-type axle (GT only at first) being adopted for the Roadster in July 1967.

The MGB GT (permanent coupe, two doors and hatchback) was launched in October 1965.

The MGB was always a commercial success – with 23,308 built in the first full production calendar year (1963) and with 26,542 the following year, it was already Abingdon's best-selling machine. These achievements were paralleled by its reception in North America. In 1963, 15,054 cars were sent to North America and 16,753 in 1964.

In 1966, with the MGB GT now on stream, total production was 32,916, of which 20,394 were destined for North America. Not even the cheaper, smaller, twin-badged Sprite/Midget cars could sell at this rate, so clearly the MGB and MGB GT were exactly right for their marketplace – and there was more to come in the years that followed.

- Black
- Sandy Beige (GT only)
- Iris Blue
- Mineral Blue
- British Racing Green

- Chelsea Grey
- Grampian Grey (GT only)
- Tartan Red
- Old English White

- Pale Primrose Yellow
- Metallic Golden Beige (GT only)
- Metallic Riviera Silver Blue (GT only)

ACCESSORIES

MAJOR OPTIONS ONLY:

- Engine oil cooler (standard on export, standard in UK from late 1964)
- Radio
- Heater/demister (standard for export)
- Radial-ply tyres (from 1965)

- Tonneau cover (Roadster)
- Anti-roll bar (Roadster until November 1966, GT never)
- Folding soft-top mechanism
- Overdrive
- Removable hardtop (Roadster)

RIVALS

By the time the MGB arrived in 1962, the marketplace was well-stocked with rival sports cars. The MGA of 1955–62 had been a fine car, which had only encouraged MG's rivals to produce similar machines of their own.

At first, the principal competition came from Triumph, and to a lesser extent from Sunbeam, though Fiat chimed in from late 1966, and Alfa Romeo (with the Giulietta and later the Guilia Spider) was always a factor.

Because Triumph had established its TR2 in North America as early as 1954 – which was even before the MGA had been launched – it was the MGB's major, head-to-head, competitor. The latest TR, the Michelotti-styled TR4 (but still with a separate chassis frame), had been on sale for a year when the MGB appeared. Apart from its crashingly hard ride, it was a very competent competitor. It had a slightly larger engine (2,138cc), and cost a little more, but had a roomy cockpit. The MGB could not match features such as face-level ventilation and the two-piece optional hardtop, but it still shaded the Triumph in sporting pedigree.

From early 1965 the TR4 gave way to the TR4A, a car in which all-independent suspension was standard (except in the USA where it was still optional). In the mid-1960s, TR sales averaged 12,000–15,000 cars a year, a figure which was never more than half that of the MGB.

Although it was physically smaller, from late 1966 the original Triumph GT6 was a rival for the MGB GT, as it had a 95bhp/2-litre six-cylinder engine, a 100+mph (160+km/h) top speed, and a smart but cramped coupe/hatchback cabin. Although the price was right – a GT6 cost £985 when an MGB GT cost £1,016 – the Triumph was let down by poor handling from its swing-axle rear suspension.

The Sunbeam Alpine – pretty, with tail fins, though heavier and not as fast – was an important newcomer to this market sector. New in 1959, by 1962 this monocoque two-seater was Series II, in 80bhp/1,592cc guise. Then, in rapid succession, came the Series III of 1963, the clipped-fin Series IV of 1964, and finally the 92.5bhp/1,725cc Series V of 1965. At best, the Alpine sold less than 10,000 cars per year, only one-third that of the MGB.

As far as the MGB Mk I was concerned, the 90bhp/1.4-litre/five-speed gearbox Fiat 124 Spider was only a minor influence, as it did not go on sale until 1966–67. Even so, its specification was threatening, for sexy Pininfarina styling was mixed in with a twin overhead-camshaft engine *and* a longer wheelbase 2+2 coupe derivative.

Never built in right-hand-drive form, the Spider would become a serious rival in North America, while the coupe was a rival everywhere. There would be better/larger-engined types in the future.

Also with twin-cam engines and five-speed gearboxes, the twin Alfa Romeos – 1.3 and 1.6-litre Giulietta Spiders until 1966, 1.6-litre Spiders thereafter – were mechanically sophisticated, but though the Americans loved their image, they did not like their prices or their reputation for early rusting (for which BMC was very grateful).

Although this market sector would change considerably in future years, for MG it was always highly competitive.

ENGINE

Layout	Four-cylinder, in-line
Block material	Cast iron
Head material	Cast iron
Peak power	95bhp (net) @ 5,400rpm
Peak torque	110lb ft @ 3,000rpm
Bore	80.26mm
Stroke	88.9mm
Cubic capacity	1,798cc
Compression ratio	8.8:1

FUEL SUPPLY

Carburettors	SU constant vacuum
Type	2 × HS4
Fuel pump	SU electric

ELECTRICAL

Earth	Positive
Battery	2 × 58AH 6-volt
Generator	C/40-1 dynamo
Starter motor	Lucas M418G

TRANSMISSION

Clutch	Single-plate, diaphragm spring
Clutch diameter	8.0in (20cm)
Gearbox type	Manual, four-speed, no synchromesh on first gear
Internal ratios	4th: 1.00; 3rd: 1.374; 2nd: 2.214; 1st: 3.636; reverse 4.755:1
Overall gear ratios	4th: 3.909; 3rd: 5.369; 2nd: 8.656; 1st: 14.214; reverse 18.588:1
Optional overdrive (and ratio)	Laycock D-Type, 0.802:1
Overall ratios with overdrive	O/D 4th: 3.135; 4th: 3.909; O/D 3rd: 4.306; 3rd: 5.369; 2nd: 8.656; 1st: 14.214, reverse 18.588:1

BRAKES

Front, type	Lockheed disc, hydraulic
Front, size	10.75in diameter
Rear, type	Lockheed drum, hydraulic
Rear, size	10 × 1.75in

STEERING

Type	Rack and pinion
Turns (L-to-L)	2.9
Turning circle	32ft 6in (10m) approx. between kerbs

FRONT SUSPENSION

Type	Independent, coil springs, wishbones, on separate pressed-steel cross member
Anti-roll bar	Optional on Roadsters at first (standard from November 1966); standard on GT
Dampers	Lever arm, hydraulic

REAR SUSPENSION

Type	Beam axle, half-elliptic leaf springs
Anti-roll bar	None
Dampers	Lever arm, hydraulic

WHEELS AND TYRES

Wheel size	14in diameter, 4.0in rim width (Roadster) or 5.0in (GT)
Optional wire wheels	14in diameter, 4.5in rim width
Tyres	Cross-ply
Tyre size	5.60–14in

CAPACITIES

Engine oil	7.5 pints
Gearbox oil	4.5 pints
Gearbox + overdrive oil	5.3 pints
Rear axle oil	2.25 pints
Cooling system	9.5 pints
Fuel tank	10 Imperial gallons at first, 12.7 Imperial gallons from Mar 1965, 10 Imperial gallons (North American market) from Oct 1969

DIMENSIONS

Length	12ft 9.3in (3,894mm)
Width	4ft 11.7in (1,516mm)
Height (unladen)	Tourer 4ft 1.4in (1,255mm) GT 4ft 1.75in (1,264mm)
Wheelbase	7ft 7in (2,311mm)
Front track	4ft 1in (1,245mm)
Rear track	4ft 1.25in (1,251mm)
Ground clearance (unladen)	5in (127mm)
Weight (unladen)	Tourer 2,030lb (921kg) GT 2,190lb (993kg)

PERFORMANCE

0–60mph (0–97kph)	12.2sec
Top speed	103mph (166km/h)
Standing ¼-mile	18.7sec
Overall fuel consumption	22mpg (13ltr/100km)
Typical fuel consumption	25mpg (11ltr/100km)

Although it may look unfashionably high off the road in the 2000s, the MGB was sleek and ground-hugging by 1960s standards. The centre-lock wire spoke wheels were an optional extra – and very popular.

BELOW: The original MGB was unmistakable, the style being pleasantly rounded when viewed from any angle. Except for the wire wheels and the radio aerial, everything on this car was in standard 'as 1964' specification.

TOP: Hood up or hood down ? Most MGB enthusiasts preferred to use their cars like this. With the side windows wound up (not on this BRG car) the cockpit was surprisingly weatherproof.

ABOVE: The MGB style needed little decoration – though the chrome strip along the flanks made it look a little longer. Depending on the year the car was built, the optional wire wheels could be painted, or chrome-plated.

LEFT: Neat, tidy and absolutely 'as-built' in 1964, with chrome bumper overriders, and the octagonal MGB badge on the boot lid.

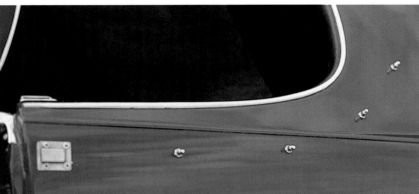

ABOVE: Because there was so much perspex panelling in the soft-top, all-round visibility was good even with the hood erect.

LEFT: The line of fasteners let in to the steel panel behind the cabin of this 1964 MGB show where the optional tonneau cover would be fitted.

BELOW: Every MGB had a swivelling front quarter-light in the doors – useful for letting in fresh air when the side windows were rolled up and the roof was erect.

TOP LEFT: Centre-lock wire spoke wheels were an optional extra from Day One. Many owners specified chrome-plated wheels which, theoretically, were not quite as strong as the painted variety – but they looked smarter. On safety grounds, knock-on ears like this were banned from some markets right from the start, and from the whole North American continent from February 1967.

TOP RIGHT: MGB headlamps were always neatly recessed – and Renault quite wrongly claimed that this design had been lifted from their Floride/Caravelle layout!

ABOVE: This chrome-plated grille was seen in every MGB and MGB GT built until the end of the 1969 Model Year. The engine oil cooler, visible behind the grille bars, was a standard fitting.

LEFT: On original MGBs there was useful space behind the seats, which was always neatly carpetted. A 'seat' cushion was an optional extra, but there was really no leg space for anyone to travel comfortably in that area of the car.

BELOW: This simple little brightwork grille covered the fresh air aperture to the heater or (in some cases) the fresh air unit, which was mounted under and ahead of it, in front of the passenger bulkhead.

The MGB Mk I had a simple but well-fitted-out cockpit. The seats had contrasting-colour piping and there was a fly-off handbrake, though the safety belts on this 1964 car were never fitted at the factory, and would not be compulsory until spring 1967.

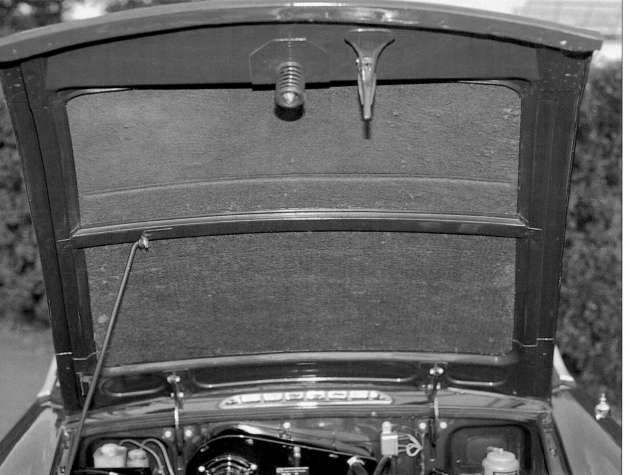

TOP: The original 'Packaway' hood frame could be dismantled and removed from its mounting position, then stowed away. Starting from scratch, they say, it took little more than a minute to get the frame out of the back, slot it into place, stretch the hood over it, and tie it all down.

ABOVE: Open Wide ! There was simple sound-deadening felt glued to the underside of the bonnet panel.

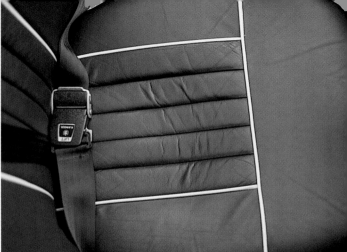

TOP LEFT: This was the original style of MGB steering wheel, with three sprung spokes. It lasted throughout the run of the MGB and GT Mk Is. In later life, many owners fitted different accessory wheels.

TOP RIGHT: This was the standard style of leather seat cover on the Mk I MGB, complete with contrast-colour piping. The Kangol static (i.e. fixed length) safety belts were a dealer-fitted option.

ABOVE: Like all BMC B-Series, the MGB engine had all its engine electrical equipment grouped on one (the right) side of the cylinder block. The heater fitted to this car was an optional extra - though most cars actually had one fitted.

ABOVE: The early MGBs had the simplest-of-all engine installations, for after this car was built the first positive crankcase breathing equipment was added on top of the tappet cover.

RIGHT: This overhead view shows how the engine oil cooler was mounted ahead of the water-cooling radiator, and just behind the front grille.

BELOW: Even on early-model MGBs like this example, there was much electrical wiring under the bonnet. The voltage regulator box is positioned ahead of the mounting for the pedals and hydraulic reservoirs.

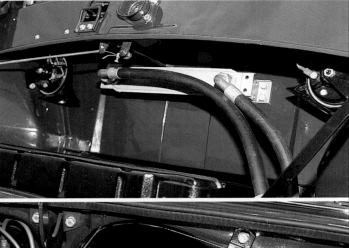

TOP: Until 1971, MGB engines were sprayed in this red colour. Note the wall-to-wall Lucas electrical fittings on this side of the engine.

ABOVE: Purely by chance, it seems, there was much empty space ahead of the MGB's cooling radiator – which would be valuable when the longer-engined MGC came along.

CHAPTER THREE

MGB Mk II

1967 to 1974

ONCE the originally planned options had arrived, the first variety of MGB – Roadster and GT – ran steadily for five years, with a settled specification and style. Development carried on, however, which meant that the MGB was finally ready for an important update in late 1967.

The revised car was unofficially known as the Mk II (though it was never badged or advertised as such), and it went on to have a complex but successful seven-year life. Several factors made the life and times of this car a lot more complicated than originally intended.

First of all, and right from the start, with the 1968 Model Year cars, MG had to cope with the onset of new and ever-tightening exhaust emission and safety/crash-test regulations in North America. Then, from January 1968, the marque found itself part of the newly-formed British Leyland combine.

Later, as the dead hand of the corporate product planners fell upon Abingdon, the team was also faced with bringing in a series of annual cosmetic facelifts, rather than getting on with the design of a replacement model, which was what they wanted to do.

Although these were turbulent times for MG (*every* subsidiary of British Leyland had to face regular upheavals, modified forward plans, rationalization proposals and abrupt policy swings during this period), the MGB continued as a major success.

Helped along by its own design stability – throughout the seven-year period, all cars had the same basic 1,798cc engine, and there was always a choice of open Roadster or closed GT body styles – Mk II production approached 220,000 in seven years. Although seven years brought changes to wheels, grilles, cockpit trim and fittings and colour

In a life of seven years, the Mk II had three slightly different front-end treatments – the original, a recessed-type grille and (from late 1972) this more traditional treatment. The metal pressings around the grille, however, were not altered.

schemes, there were no changes to the car's shape, so that a 1974 car still looked closely similar to the 1967–68 variety. Even in 1974, when the style had been in production for twelve years, this was still the accepted standard by which all other sports car reputations had to be measured.

As described below, it is clear that the Mk II was a better-specified car than the original – the all-synchromesh gearbox and the regularly updated cabin equipment specification saw to that – and it was also the time when automatic transmission became an (unsuccessful) option.

It was from the basis of this popular and effective model that the much more special six-cylinder MGC (1967–69) was produced, as well as the refined V8-engined MGB GT V8 of 1973–76. These models are described and illustrated in Chapters 5 and 6 respectively.

If impending new North American crash-test regulations had not required a major change to the front and rear bumper specifications (and the need to lift the whole car further off the ground), the Mk II might have gone on even longer. However, these new cars (together with the vastly different North American spec. engines) had to be treated, and developed, separately.

STRUCTURE

There were two major reasons for change to the familiar monocoque – one connected with the arrival of new transmissions, and the other the need to share as much of the reengineering as possible with the new six-cylinder MGC, which was a rather different structure ahead of the bulkhead.

The availability of two entirely fresh transmissions – an all-synchromesh gearbox (to be shared with the MGC and with the ADO 61 Austin 3-litre saloon) and an automatic transmission option (both of which were shared with the MGC) – meant that the transmission tunnel had to made more capacious. Compared with the original cars, therefore, the Mk II had a wider and more square-sectioned tunnel, with provision for a larger clutch bell housing.

In addition, structures for the North American market gradually became more special – not only with provision for extra side/repeater lamps and reflectors, but by making provision for three (instead of two) windscreen wipers on Roadsters for 1969. Door-strengthening bars were also included from the start-up of 1973 MY production.

In and around all this, assembly of shells was concentrated at Pressed Steel from 1969, and at a similar time the bonnet pressing became steel instead of aluminium. And, as the date sheet makes clear, no fewer than thirty-four different body colours were made available in this seven-year period!

RUNNING GEAR

Not only did the Mk II rely on the same durable BMC B-Series engine throughout its seven-year run, but it was joined by a brand new manual transmission and by the option of automatic transmission. The Salisbury-type rear axle, however, remained unchanged.

Throughout this period, all engines were built around Negative Earth electrics and alternators (see below). For North American markets, changes to deal with exhaust emission regulations saw the power drop to 82bhp/5,400rpm for 1971–74, although the official rating of all other engines stayed unchanged at 95bhp/5,400rpm.

From the outset, North American engines had air pumps injecting air into the exhaust ports, evaporative loss-control systems were installed for California for 1970 (all North America for 1971), and low (8.0:1) compression ratios for 1972. Carburettor specs changed too – from HS4s (original) to HIF4s (1972 on). Engines for the UK market had an easier time, with HS4 carburettors fitted until 1973 and HIF4s thereafter, and with a 9.0:1 compression from 1972 onwards.

The manual transmission was a totally new four-speed, all-synchromesh design which, since it was laid down to cope with much more powerful six-cylinder engines, was very robust and easily able to cope with B-Series power. Although different in every way – new casing, new gear wheels, new components – its internal ratios were very similar indeed to those of the now-obsolete 'crash-first' box. Because it also had a different remote control gear-change arrangement, the position of the change speed lever itself was new – for it now protruded vertically from the transmission tunnel.

As before, overdrive was optional (and, when fitted, worked on top and third gears) – but this time it was a more modern type, the Laycock LH, with a step-up ratio of 0.82:1. The majority of all MGBs seem to have had this option fitted, although it would not be standardized until part way through the run of the *next* MGB derivative.

The offering of an automatic transmission option was a real surprise – this being the well-known Borg Warner Type 35 box, which had a torque converter and three forward ratios. Automatic, however, took the edge off the car's performance, and it was not popular (incidentally, it was never actively marketed in North America). Between 1967 and 1973, when the option was finally dropped, only 1,737 MGB Automatics were ever sold – of which 1,346 were sold in the UK, the majority of them being fitted to GTs.

Since the last of the 'banjo' B-Series axles had been fitted to an MGB in early 1967, only the more sturdy Salisbury-type of back axle was ever fitted to the Mk II – with a 3.909:1 ratio for manual transmission cars and 3.70:1 for automatic.

SUSPENSION, STEERING AND BRAKES

Compared with the original MGB, the MGB Mk II's 'chassis' was changed only in detail. Following the update in 1966, all cars were therefore fitted with a front anti-roll torsion bar as standard.

Spring and damper settings were as before, except that from August 1972 the free length of the front coil springs was changed to raise the ride height of the front end of the car by approximately 0.5in (12mm).

Compared with the Mk I, there was no change to the rear suspension. Nor were any changes made to the steering rack, although a whole variety of different steering column locks (different market destinations, different suppliers) appeared – for Finland, Germany and Sweden from the outset, Austria from January 1968, and often (but not always) to North American cars from the start of production. Steering column locks became compulsory for North America from 1970 MY onwards, and for British market cars from 1 January 1971.

There were five different types of steering wheel – the original sprung-spoke variety until late 1969, an alloy-spoke-plus-holes type for 1970, the same thing but with centre horn push for 1971, then a different style with spoke slots instead of holes for 1973, and finally deletion of the slots from June 1973.

The Lockheed brakes were much as before, though a vacuum servo became optional on single hydraulic circuit cars (i.e. not North America) from

February 1970; it became standard on UK models for the 1974 MY. Dual circuitry was adopted for North American cars from August 1968.

Except for changes to wheel nuts (disc *and* wheels), there was no change to wheel specifications at first (perforated disc or painted centre- lock wires were always available). However, for the 1970 MY, a new four-spoke style of Rostyle disc wheel became standard, these continuing to the end of the run.

Dunlop radial-ply tyres (165–14in) were optional to the normal 5.60–14in cross-plys at first, but were standardized in August 1973.

ELECTRICAL EQUIPMENT

Compared with the original model, the major electrical change on the Mk II was that a Negative Earth 12-volt system was adopted, with all components provided by Lucas. This meant, of course, that almost every instrument, control box and engine electrical item was different from before.

Storage power was still provided by a pair of 6-volt batteries, wired in series, which were carried in cradles mounted ahead of the line of the rear axle, one each side of the propeller shaft and accessed by a removable plate in the bodyshell floor.

For Mk II cars, power was provided by a alternating-current alternator – a Lucas 16AC at first, but a later 16ACR type from the beginning of 1969 models, and by a larger 17ACR from February 1973. A Lucas M418G pre-engaged starter was standard on all models until the end of 1971 MY production, after which it was replaced by a 2M100 type.

COCKPIT AND TRIM

When the Mk II was introduced in late 1967, the original facia/instrument/equipment style was retained on all but North American market cars. At this juncture, LHD North American market cars received a new facia, which had a vast padded screen rail (the 'Abingdon pillow') and a different layout of instruments.

In styling, though not in technical terms, there were frequent changes over the years, and it is best to summarize these by Model Year introductions (these usually being made in the autumn – so a 1971 MY car would start its production life in autumn 1970, for instance).

1969

Trim changes for 1969 saw the deletion of colour-contrast piping, while reclining seats were standardized, with control by a chrome lever to one side of the squab.

Mk Is and Mk IIs had neatly recessed headlamps, with lenses by Lucas. Over the years, several slight pattern changes were made, but replacements are easy to find today.

- Aqua (turquoise)
- Black
- Antelope Beige (GT only)
- Bedouin (beige)
- Blaze (orange)
- Sandy Beige (GT only)
- Bermuda Blue (GT only)
- Midnight Blue
- Mineral Blue
- Blue Royale
- Teal Blue
- Bracken (brown)

- British Racing Green
- Limeflower (green)
- Green Mallard
- New Racing Green
- Tundra (green)
- Grampian Grey (GT only)
- Harvest Gold
- Mirage (mauve)
- Mustard
- Aconite (purple)
- Black Tulip (purple)
- Damask Red

- Flame Red
- Tartan Red
- Glacier White
- Old English White
- Snowberry White
- Bronze Yellow
- Citron (yellow)
- Pale Primrose Yellow
- Metallic Golden Beige (GT only)
- Metallic Riviera Silver Blue (GT only)

MAJOR OPTIONS ONLY:

- Engine oil cooler (standard on export, standard in UK from late 1964)
- Radio
- Heater/demister (standard for export except hot climates, standard for UK from late 1968)
- Radial-ply tyres (from 1965) – then standard from 1973

- Tonneau cover (Roadster) – then standard on UK market cars from August 1972
- Anti-roll bar (Roadster until November 1966) then standard: always standard on GT
- Folding soft-top mechanism (until August 1970, then standard)
- Overdrive
- Removable hardtop (Roadster)

1970

A very 'non-Abingdon'-type of radiator grille was adopted, recessed into the intake. Inside the car, the trim of seating was henceforth in Ambla (plastic) instead of leather.

The North American market padded facia was adopted for German and Swedish market cars.

1971

From August 1970, a new type of Michelotti-designed foldaway soft-top/hood became standard. Rubber-faced overriders were standardized.

From January 1971, Kangol static seat belts were fitted at the factory, instead of by dealers.

1972

Facia modifications included the adoption of fresh-air vents in the centre of the facia. North American cars gained a glovebox, plus a between-seats console that was also fitted to all cars.

North American market cars had inertia reel belts as standard.

1973

There was a return to a traditional type of grille, though it was not that of the first cars.

The previously optional tonneau cover became standard from January 1973 on home market cars (but was still optional on North American market models).

1974

For 1974, North American market cars were inflicted with large energy-absorbing rubber overriders.

PRODUCTION

Except for the first two years there was some mix-and-match assembly concerning the MGC at Abingdon, the MGB Mk II was initially put together in exactly the same sequence as the original cars.

Until 1969, painted and trimmed bodyshells came from Morris Bodies Branch, Coventry (Roadster), and from Pressed Steel/Cowley Bodies Plant (GT), but from 1969 (thought to be for the

MGB MK II – 1967 TO 1974

start-up of 1970 MY cars) Roadster assembly was taken out of Coventry and returned to Swindon/ Cowley as well. The new all-synchromesh gearbox came from Longbridge, while the optional three-speed automatic transmission came from Borg Warner of South Wales.

As ever with these cars, there was very little mechanization of assembly at Abingdon, for although there were at least three parallel MGB assembly lines (such was the demand), there was no powered method of moving cars from station to station – just good, Abingdon manpower.

CAREER

Except that, as part of the new British Leyland regime, the MGB Mk II received a series of regular Model Year cosmetic facelifts, it had a steady and totally predictable life at Abingdon, and was always the most numerous car to be built there, for it always outsold the Sprite/Midget and MGC lines.

There were no major style changes in its seven-year life, and mechanically the only major change was to phase out the automatic transmission option in August 1973 before the start-up of 1974 MY assembly.

From 1967 to 1974, the production achievements were as in the box below:

Rostyle pressed steel wheels of this type were adopted as standard equipment from the beginning of 1970 Model Year, and would carry on, virtually unaltered, to the end of the MGB's life.

	ROADSTER	GT
1967	560	329
1968	17,247	8,349
1969	18,887	12,135
1970	23,662	12,510
1971	22,511	12,169
1972	26,222	13,171
1973	19,546	10,208
1974	19,582	9,168

PRODUCTION	MGB Mk II
DATES	October 1967–September 1974
CHASSIS NUMBERS	138800–360300 (Roadster)
	139824–361000 (GT)
PRODUCTION BREAK POINTS	Facelift/1970 MY 187211
	Facelift/1971 MY 219000
	Facelift/1972 MY 258001
	Start of 1973 MY 294251
	Start of 1974 MY 328101
TOTAL PRODUCED	142,410 Roadster
	76,402 GT

MGB MK II (Chrome Bumpers)

ENGINE

Layout	Four-cylinder, in-line
Block material	Cast iron
Head material	Cast iron
Peak power (UK)	95bhp (net) @ 5,400rpm
Peak torque (UK)	110lb ft @ 3,000rpm
Peak power	82bhp (DIN) @ 5,400rpm (North America, 1971 on)
Peak torque	97lb ft @ 2,900rpm (North America, 1971 on)
Bore	80.26mm
Stroke	88.9mm
Cubic capacity	1,798cc
Compression ratio	8.8:1

FUEL SUPPLY

Carburettors	SU constant vacuum
Type	2 × HS4 at first
	2 × HIF4 (Export, from 1971, UK from 1973)
Fuel pump	SU electric

ELECTRICAL

Earth	Negative
Battery	2 × 58AH 6-volt
Generator	Lucas alternating-current alternator – 16AC at first, then 16ACR (1969) and 17ACR (1973)
Starter motor	Lucas, pre-engaged

MANUAL TRANSMISSION

Clutch	Single-plate, diaphragm spring
Clutch diameter	8.0in (20cm)
Gearbox type	Manual, four-speed, all-synchromesh
Internal ratios	4th: 1.00; 3rd: 1.382; 2nd: 2.167; 1st: 3.440; reverse: 3.067:1
Overall gear ratios	4th: 3.909; 3rd: 5.402; 2nd: 8.470; 1st: 13.446; reverse: 12.098:1
Optional overdrive	Laycock LH-Type, 0.82:1 (and ratio)
Overall ratios with	O/D 4th: 3.205; 4th: 3.909; O/D 3rd: 4.429; overdrive 3rd: 5.402; 2nd: 8.470; 1st: 13.446; reverse: 12.098:1

AUTOMATIC TRANSMISSION (1967 to 1973 only)

Type	Borg Warner Type 35
	Three forward ratios, plus torque converter
Internal ratios	Top: 1.00; intermediate: 1.45; low: 2.39; reverse: 2.09:1
Overall ratios	Top: 3.70; intermediate: 5.365; low: 8.843; reverse: 7.733:1

BRAKES

Front, type	Lockheed disc, hydraulic
Front, size	10.75in diameter
Rear, type	Lockheed drum, hydraulic
Rear, size	10 × 1.75in

STEERING

Type	Rack and pinion
Turns (L-to-L)	2.9
Turning circle	32ft 6in (10m) approx. between kerbs

FRONT SUSPENSION

Type	Independent, coil springs, wishbones, on separate pressed-steel cross member
Anti-roll bar	Standard
Dampers	Lever arm, hydraulic

REAR SUSPENSION

Type	Beam axle, half-elliptic leaf springs
Anti-roll bar	None
Dampers	Lever arm, hydraulic

WHEELS AND TYRES

Wheel size	14in diameter, 4.0in rim width (Roadster) or 5.0in (GT) – 4.5 in Rostyle style from 1969
Optional wire wheels	14in diameter, 4.5in. rim width
Tyres	Cross-ply (Radial-ply from 1973)
Tyre size	5.60–14in (165–14)

CAPACITIES

Engine oil	6.0 pints
Gearbox oil	5.0 pints
Gearbox + overdrive oil	6.0 pints
Rear axle oil	1.5 pints
Cooling system	10.0 pints
Fuel tank	12.7 Imperial gallons, 10.0 Imperial gallons for North American market from October 1969

DIMENSIONS

Length	12ft 9.3in (3,894mm)
Width	4ft 11.7in (1,516mm)
Height (unladen):	Tourer 4ft 1.4in (1,255mm)
	GT 4ft 1.75in (1,264mm)
Wheelbase	7ft 7in (2,311mm)
Front track	4ft 1in (1,245mm)
Rear track	4ft 1.25in (1,251mm)
Ground clearance (unladen)	5in (127mm)
Weight (unladen)	Tourer 2,140lb (970kg)
	GT 2,260lb (1,025kg)

PERFORMANCE (UK)

0–60mph (0–97kph)	12.2sec
Top speed	103mph (166km/h)
Standing ¼-mile	18.7sec
Overall fuel consumption	22mpg (13ltr/100km)
Typical fuel consumption	25mpg (11ltr/100km)

CKD (Completely Knocked Down) assembly of GTs, which was always very limited, ended in 1971, the last CKD Roadsters being built in 1972. GT assembly for North America carried on, at full speed, until the end of the run of this model, but ended thereafter, for no 'rubber bumper' GTs would ever be sent to North America.

RIVALS

As the Mk II's career progressed, it seemed to have fewer, rather than more, rivals, a fact that may have been partially responsible for a steady increase in sales. Compared with the Mk I of 1962–67, the Mk II no longer had to contend with the Sunbeam Alpine (which had been dropped early in 1968), while the already expensive Alfa Romeo Giulia Spider eased up to 2-litres and an even higher price.

Triumph competition came from two cars – the latest TR and the ever-improving GT6, though neither faced the MGB head on. Almost coincidental with the launch of the Mk II, the TR became a 2.5-litre TR5 (North America only: TR250), in which independent rear suspension was finally standardized. For 1969, these were further revised as TR6s, with new styling but little-changed running gear.

TR5s and rest-of-the-world TR6PIs, complete with 150bhp and fuel injection, were way too expensive, and faced up to the MGC, while even the TR250/TR6 carb. had 105bhp, and cost more than the MGB.

Because of its dodgy handling, the original six-cylinder GT6 was poor competition, but from late 1968 the Mk II had wishbone rear suspension, and was much improved. The facelifted MK III that followed in late 1970, was an even better car, but fell out of favour with British Leyland in 1973 and was dropped later that year. A 1973 MGT GT cost £1,547, and the GT6 Mk III cost £1,353.

The Fiat 124 Spider and coupe models 'grew up' in this period, first with 90bhp/1.4-litre twin-cam engines, then to 110bhp/1.6-litres with a front-end restyle in late 1969, and finally to a full 118/1.8-litre size in late 1972. A full 2-litre size would follow in 1978 when the 'rubber bumper' MGB was on sale, though only in the Spider, for the coupe was to be discontinued in 1975.

This model was always serious MGB competition – as an example, in the USA in 1968 the MGB GT cost $3,160 at a time when the 124 Sport Coupe cost $2,924 and the 124 Spider cost $3,226. At the end of the 1960s Fiat was building 50,000 of these cars in a year – more than the MGB – and for a short time it outsold the MGB in North America too. Fortunately for MG, the Fiat's propensity for early rusting soon harmed its reputation.

ABOVE: This Pale Primrose Yellow MGB is absolutely typical of Mk IIs of the period. In fact this car is something of a hybrid, and slightly non-standard, for it is a 1970-model which should have had the recessed front grille, yet the owner has reverted to the original, traditional style instead. The wire spoke wheels, of course, were optional extras, as were other features such as the radio installation, the driving lamps and the luggage grid.

LEFT: Except for the club badges, this Teal Blue 1973-model MGB GT is absolutely standard, for the rubber-tipped overriders were standardized on 1971 Model Year cars.

OPPOSITE PAGE
Yet another variation on a theme – a 1974 Model Mk II, a car built in the last season before the black-bumper nose was adopted.

OPPOSITE PAGE

Classic car detectives will love this one – an MGB Mk II built in 1970 Model Year, but registered in 1970/1971, and retrofitted with a grille from a 1962–1967 model ! Still a handsome and well-loved example, though.

THIS PAGE

ABOVE: Pale Primrose Yellow was a very becoming colour on MGB Mk IIs like this one, but was only available from 1967 to 1970 Model Year cars.

BELOW: Some owners liked to customize their MGBs - this early-1970s Mk II having flared wheelarches, Minilite-style alloy road wheels, no front bumper, revised front sheet metal, and a special colour scheme.

MGB Mk II – 1967 to 1974

TOP: Any MGB Mk II owner ambitious enough to go off on long holidays could invest in a luggage bootrack. Such racks were available as officially-approved accessories from BMC dealerships.

ABOVE: Anyone who buys an MGB, and does not join a one-make club is ill-advised! The owner of this 1973 model is playing it safe by being a member of both the MG Owners' Club (red badge) and the long-established MG Car Club.

LEFT: Did one really need to be told that this Mk II was an MGB GT – for this must be one of the best-known styles in the world? In every detail, incidentally, the electrical equipment of this 1973 model is correct for the period.

ABOVE: This luggage rack is absolutely typical of the type of period accessory correctly applied to latter-day Mk IIs. Sensibly (for load-carrying purposes) it is tied into the hinges at the front of the boot lid.

LEFT: Both for style, and for extra security, rubber-tipped bumpers were fitted to UK-market cars from the start of the 1971 Model Year.

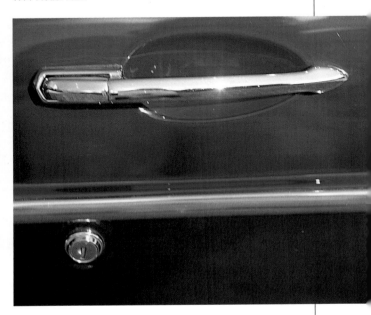

ABOVE: Push-button door handles, with remote locks, were standardized on the MGB during 1965, and were fitted throughout the life of the Mk II – in fact until the MGB was discontinued in 1980.

ABOVE: For the last two seasons of Mk II assembly – 1973 and 1974 Model Years, in fact – MGBs had this type of radiator grille, the third (of four) which the model would have in an 18 year life.

BELOW: This type of swivelling front quarter light on this Mk II was typical of those fitted to all MGBs, and would not be altered again throughout the MGB's long life.

OPPOSITE PAGE

TOP LEFT: The combination of the MG and BGT badges was one of the proudest in the British motor industry for many years. This style was adopted for 1973 Model Year cars, and continued until the end, in 1980.

TOP RIGHT: On the door trims, this type of black plastic pull-to-release handle, with a separate pull handle, was new with the Mk II, and would feature until the end of MGB production.

BOTTOM: From mid-1971, new-build MGB engines were painted black, instead of red. Also visible on this 1973-model is the alternator which supplied power on all Mk II and later MGB models.

ABOVE: Even in 1973 there was still a lot of spare space ahead of the four-cylinder MGB's radiator, and as ever the engine oil cooler lived spaciously ahead of the radiator, just behind the grille.

A Lucas alternator was always standard on Mk II and later MGBs – a 16AC at first, a 16ACR for 1969, and a 17ACR (this unit) for 1973 Model Year and afterward.

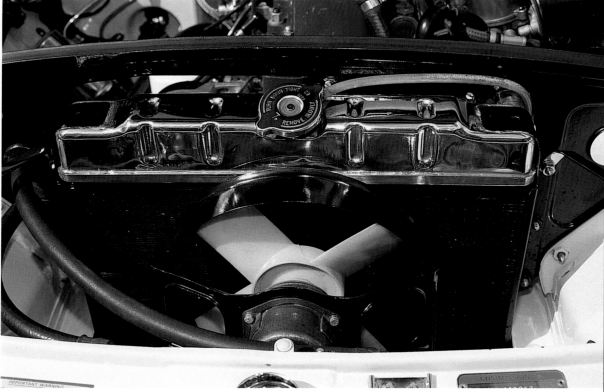

TOP: Compared with the original 1962-type MGB, the 1970-model MGB was beginning to take on extra pipes and wires. Concertina-type water hoses had also taken over as standard equipment.

BOTTOM: More modification and upgrading – but in a very tasteful and practical manner – this 1970 Mk II has been treated to an extra (electrically-driven) cooling fan ahead of the radiator, and the paint has been stripped from the top of the radiator itself, exposing the brass, ready to be polished.

ABOVE: This type of alloy-spoked steering wheel, complete with pierced slots, was only fitted to Home Market MGB Mk IIs built in the 1973 Model Year, after which solid spokes were adopted instead. The air vents in the centre of the facia had arrived with the start of 1972 Model Year assembly.

BELOW: From the start of 1972 Model Year assembly, Home Market Mk IIs had a facia like this, complete with centrally positioned air vents, and with provision for an (optional dealer extra) radio to be fitted in a centre panel below them.

CHAPTER FOUR

MGB Mk II
Black-Bumper Model

1974 to 1980

AS almost every MG enthusiast will agree, from the mid-1970s the MGB was living on borrowed time. Not only had British Leyland made it clear that no funds would be made available to develop a replacement model, but the MG design staff were always under pressure to keep up with the ever-changing, ever-tightening requirements of North American legislators. After 1975, the major improvements made to MGBs were confined to colour schemes, decoration and to produce 'special editions'.

Starting in the autumn of 1974, the MGB's looks were significantly changed because big, black polyurethane-coated bumpers had to be adopted to meet new crash tests, and in North America the car's performance was quite ruined because the engine had to be radically detuned to meet the exhaust emission rules. At first, too, the handling was impaired because the ride height had to be lifted to get the new bumpers to a regulation-meeting level, this deficiency not being overcome for two years until a new handling package was finally made ready.

The effect of all these changes was to make late model MGBs slower, heavier and less well-handling than before, yet despite this sales held up remarkably well. This achievement was even more praiseworthy when one remembers that another arm of

From late 1974, all MGBs were fitted with these large, black polyurethane bumpers. This car is a UK-market LE, and therefore also carries an under-bumper front spoiler.

British Leyland had produced the new Triumph TR7 at the same time, a car which had not only got all the development capital, but a great deal of marketing attention too.

Whether one likes to admit it or not, this was a period of slow decline for the MGB, so the miracle is that Abingdon's morale stayed high – until an announcement of the factory's impending closure was made in September 1979.

It was also a period of retrenchment in export markets. 'Black bumper' MGB GTs were never exported to North America, and apart from North American deliveries there were no left-hand-drive MGB exports of any type after 1976. The last MGB GT V8 was also completed in the autumn of 1976. CKD (Completely Knocked Down) exports had already ended in 1973, and the only export market to be opened up was to Japan, where 739 Roadsters were delivered between 1977 and 1980.

Even so, in the first year of 'black bumper' production, no fewer than 24,688 cars were produced, followed by 28,681 in 1977. Serious decline began in 1979 when a proposal to re-engine the car with the much more powerful (and 'clean') 'O'-Series engine was cancelled, and the last MGB of all was assembled on 23 October 1980.

This marked the end of a remarkable car's amazing career, for the MGB family had been in production for more than twenty-eight years, during which time 523,836 cars of all types – 512,243 of them being four-cylinder cars – had been made. This set an MG record and also a British sports car record, which is unlikely to be beaten.

STRUCTURE

To meet new crash-test regulations in North America (where more than 90 per cent of Roadster production was destined to go), the familiar monocoque had to be re-engineered and repositioned for 1975 and beyond. Even though it had been decided that from this time the MGB GT would not be sent to North America, the same package of changes was made for the sake of commonization. These changes took two main forms – to provide better barrier crash protection and to raise the entire shell further off the deck, the latter being done by providing lengthened rear spring hangers and a modified front cross member.

To accommodate the vast new bumpers, outer front and rear wing pressings had to be changed, while a more subtle change was that the junction between the rear valance and the rear wing pressing was also moved outboard. At the same time, all shells were altered to accommodate the cradle for the single 12-volt battery (*see* section on Electrical Equipment, p.47).

For 1976 MY there were reinforcements to the front inner wheel arch panels, and for 1977 MY there were further changes in this area brought about by the movement forward of the radiator, while underbody fixings were added for the new rear anti-roll bar. No major changes to the doors, or to their internal reinforcement, were made in this period.

The bumpers themselves, though often described as 'rubber bumpers', were actually made from polyurethane, with sturdy steel armatures moulded inside them. No matter what the body colour chosen, these bumpers were always finished in gloss black. Incidentally, for the two major Limited Edition runs – for North America and for Home Market LE models in 1979–80 – there was always a substantial under-nose hard-rubber front spoiler.

This picture tells two stories – it shows off how large and carefully shaped was the polyurethane bumper fitted to MGBs from late 1974, and it also illustrates that LE models (this car) also had an under-bumper front spoiler.

RUNNING GEAR

Although (compared with the last of the 1974 'chrome bumper' cars) there were no major changes to the engine, transmission and rear axle designs, the engine came in for a great deal of detail change.

The vast majority of 1974–80 MGBs went to North America, so this version of the MGB came in for the most attention. From the start of 1975 calendar year deliveries, in addition to all the existing anti-smog gear that included air injection, the latest B-Series engine had a single 175CD5T Zenith-Stromberg carburettor (with automatic choke), along with exhaust gas recirculation, and the ability to run on lead-free fuel. Peak power was much less than before – a mere 65bhp at 4,600rpm, with top speed reduced to only 90mph (145km/h).

A catalytic converter was fitted to Californian cars from mid-1975, then to North American market cars for all States from the start of 1976 MY assembly, which meant that lead-free fuel had to be used; Canadian-market cars never got a catalytic converter.

This engine tune basically continued to the end, but was eventually joined by a cat's cradle of extra fuel circuitry, filters, cut-off valves, absorption canisters and the like, none of which were ever needed on UK market machines. Underneath all this, of course, was a small-valve B-Series engine that could just, and only just, cope.

The four-speed all-synchromesh gearbox was basically the same as on 1967–74 models, except that at first there was a higher first gear ratio (3.036:1 internal ratio compared with 3.440:1), although this was altered once again (to 3.333:1) from June 1976, the start-up of 1977 MY cars.

As on the previous (Mk II) model, the overdrive fitment was the Laycock LH design, with a step-up ratio of 0.82:1. Overdrive was standardized on all right-hand-drive cars from June 1976, but remained optional on North American market cars. At first, it operated on top and third gears, but from February 1977 (North America only) it only operated on top gear.

There was no automatic transmission option on this version of the MGB, the option having been dropped in 1973 on the previous model. As on all previous manual transmission models of the MGB, with or without overdrive, the final-drive ratio was 3.909:1.

SUSPENSION, STEERING AND BRAKES

Because the entire monocoque had to be lifted 1.5in (38mm) further off the ground when the 'rubber bumper' format was adopted, this meant wholesale detail changes to the suspension.

To gain the extra front ground clearance, the V8-type front cross member (which was already plated to provide 'padding') was added, there were new coil springs and (until June 1976, the start of 1977 MY assembly) the front anti-roll bar of the Roadster (but not the GT) was deleted. At the rear, there were longer leaf-spring hangers, which meant that the springs were more remote from the bodyshell, while the rear dampers and their linkage were modified. The rack and pinion steering was not altered, and from 1974–76 the existing alloy-spoke steering wheel was retained.

This, frankly, provided a car which did not handle as well as previous MGBs had done, there being much more body roll on corners than before. Frustrated as they were, the MG designers could do nothing about the latest car's ground clearance, but from June 1976 (and the start of 1977 MY assembly), they introduced a new package. Not

only was the front anti-roll bar reinstated on all Roadsters, but a new *rear* anti-roll bar was also specified (no previous MGB, MGC or MGB GT V8 had ever had one of these), which made a marked difference to the handling. This point saw the adoption of an entirely new type of four-spoke steering wheel, with the spokes aligned, effectively, in an 'H-formation on its side' design.

The wheel/tyre choices, as finalized on pre-1975 cars, were continued. Rostyle disc wheels were standard and centre-lock, wire-spoke wheels were optional, with 165–14in radial-ply tyres (nylon braced to early 1978, steel-braced thereafter) as standard. Gold-plated V8-type composite alloy centre/steel rim wheels were fitted to the 'Jubilee' GTs of 1975.

The exception (and make no mistake, there was often 'an exception' on MGBs), was that five-spoke cast alloy wheels were fitted to North American and British 'LE' Limited Edition types. 'Jubilee' models had 175–14in, and cast alloy-wheeled types had 185/70–14 tyres.

Compared with the above, except for the adoption of a brake servo as standard on North American market Roadsters, the braking specification was a paragon of consistency, with the original (1975 MY) cars showing no important changes from the last of the chrome bumper cars, and with no major changes made during the life of the car.

ELECTRICAL EQUIPMENT

Compared with previous MGBs, the important alteration, made at the outset, was that *this* MGB used a single 12-volt battery. This was mounted in a cradle under the floor of the bodyshell, behind the seats.

This five-spoke cast alloy wheel is best remembered as standard equipment on the 1979–80 North American market Limited Edition cars, and on the late 1980 UK-market LEs, but it was a normal optional extra at that time.

Early 'rubber bumper' cars generated power from a 17ACR alternator (which had a built-in regulator), this being upgraded to 18ACR from June 1976 and the start-up of 1977 MY assembly. As on the last of the chrome bumper cars, a Lucas 2M100 pre-engaged starter was fitted to all varieties.

All cars, for all markets, had one of various types of combined ignition/steering column lock fittings on the steering column.

COCKPIT AND TRIM

The original 'rubber bumper' cars of 1975 and 1976 had much the same type, standard and equipment of interior trim, carpets and seating as those of the last chrome bumper types, though safety belts were finally included in the list price. RHD home market cars got the GT V8-type of smaller instrument facia style and the same column stalk controls.

There was an updated range of paint/trim combinations for 1975 and 1976, a further revised set for 1977, and yet more permutations for the 1978–80 period. The 751 'Jubilee' limited-edition GTs of 1975 not only had a unique Racing Green plus gold striping paint job, gold-painted cast alloy wheels, but the interior had headrests as standard, and a full carpet specification interior.

The final, and important, trim/decoration overhaul came in June 1976, for the start-up of 1977 MY assembly. Not only was there a full carpet specification, but an entirely fresh facia layout for both RHD and LHD cars. Because of North American safety regulations, the two styles were very different, but Triumph Spitfire instruments were adopted to ease commonality problems. There were also new types of centre consoles, plus a new type of four-spoke 'safety' steering wheel. Even to the end, although there was styled provision for a radio to be fitted, this was never standard, but was an after-market option fitted by dealers or by the customers themselves.

PRODUCTION

By the time the 'rubber bumper' was introduced, the production and assembly process had settled into a familiar routine. A few changes had to be made to accommodate the slightly bulkier bodyshells.

Increasingly, however, two different types of MGB were being built. From 1975 all cars which were destined for North America were equipped with single-carburettor engines and a variety of extra safety fittings and electrical equipment. On the other hand, the GT version of this model was never exported to North America – and the last left-hand-drive cars of any type were made in 1976

Even in 1975, the MGB was much the most numerous of all cars being built at Abingdon, with no fewer than three parallel assembly lines being devoted to the model. For a while, the MGB GT V8 (see Chapter 6) was built on its own dedicated assembly track. Indeed, once the last Midget had been produced in late 1979, the MGB was the *only* car still being assembled at Abingdon.

CAREER

This, the third basic version of the MGB, had a six-year life at Abingdon. Its exterior style did not change, and the marketing emphasis became increasingly concentrated on North America. For interest, here are the important change points:

- October 1974: introduction; special single-carburettor engine for North American market cars.

- April 1975: production of 751 'Jubilee GT' models – BRG with gold striping.

- June 1975: overdrive standardized on all home market cars.

PRODUCTION		MGB Mk II
DATES	October 1974–October 2000	
CHASSIS NUMBERS	360301–523001 (Roadster)	
	361001–523002 (GT)	
PRODUCTION BREAK POINTS	Revised suspension/facia (Autumn 1976) from 410001	
TOTAL PRODUCED	Polyurethane bumpers: 128.653 Roadster	
	27.045 GT	

- Black
- Pageant Blue
- Tahiti Blue
- Bracken (brown)
- Russet Brown
- Bronze Metallic
  (1980 LE Roadster only)
- Brooklands Green

- New Racing Green
- Tundra (green)
- Harvest Gold
- Pewter Metallic
  (1980 LE GT only)
- Damask Red
- Carmine (red)
- Flamenco (red)
- Vermilion (red)

- Sandglow
- Snapdragon
- Glacier White
- Leyland White
- Bronze Yellow
- Chartreuse (yellow)
- Citron (yellow)
- Inca Yellow

ACCESSORIES

MAJOR OPTIONS ONLY:

- Radio
- Tonneau cover (Roadster) – standard for UK, then standard for North America from December 1977

- Wire wheels
- Overdrive (standard on RHD cars from 1976)
- Removable hardtop (Roadster) – no longer listed for UK from 1976

- June 1976: end of left-hand-drive MGB GT assembly; introduction of completely new facia style (RHD) and different new facia style for North American market models.

- September 1977: start-up of Japanese market production.

- March 1979: start-up of North American 'Limited Edition' models.

- August/September 1980: assembly of home market LE models.

- October 1980: end of MGB assembly.

Along with the above, a vigorous marketing policy kept the car rolling remarkably well. In six years, no fewer than 155,698 four-cylinder MGBs were built – considerably more, that is, than the much-hyped Triumph TR7 which was at once its major marketplace *and* in-house rival.

Although the production records of the early 1970s were never approached, between 23,000–30,000 MGBs were produced every year from 1975–79, and even in 1980, when the forthcoming end was known, no fewer than 14,315 were completed.

The peak for this model – 29,183 – came in 1975, and if the MGB GT derivative had not already been withdrawn from North America, those achievements would have been higher still.

During the life of this model, there were three important 'Special Edition' versions of the car:

- In 1975, 751 'Jubilee GT' models were produced, all for sale on the home market.

- In 1979–80, for North America, no fewer than 6,682 Roadsters received special Black livery and equipment; these were dubbed 'Limited Edition'.

As if we needed to be told, this decal was applied to the flanks of USA Limited Edition and UK-market LEs in 1979 and 1980.

MGB MK II ('Soft Nose'/'Rubber Bumper'/Polyurethane Bumpers)

ENGINE

Layout	Four cylinder, in line
Block material	Cast iron
Head material	Cast iron
Peak power (UK)	95bhp (net) @ 5,400rpm
Peak torque (UK)	110lb.ft. @ 3,000rpm
Peak power (North America)	65bhp (DIN) @ 4,600rpm
Peak torque (North America)	92lb.ft. @ 2,500rpm
Bore	80.26mm
Stroke	88.9mm
Cubic capacity	1,798cc
Compression ratio	8.8:1

FUEL SUPPLY

Carburettors (home market):	SU constant-vacuum Type : HIF4
Carburettors: North American related markets (except 1974-built cars)	One Zenith-Stromberg and 175CD5T
Fuel pump	SU electric

ELECTRICAL

Earth	Negative
Battery	One 12-volt
Generator	Lucas alternating-current alternator – 17ACR then (from June 1976) 18ACR
Starter motor	Lucas, pre-engaged

MANUAL TRANSMISSION

Clutch	Single-plate, diaphragm spring
Clutch diameter	8.0in (20cm)
Gearbox type	Manual, four-speed, all-synchromesh
Internal ratios	4th: 1.00; 3rd: 1.382; 2nd: 2.167; 1st: 3.036; reverse: 3.067:1
Overall gear ratios	4th: 3.909; 3rd: 5.402; 2nd: 8.470; 1st: 11.867; reverse: 12.098:1
Optional overdrive (and ratio)	Laycock LH-Type, 0.82:1
Overall ratios with	O/D 4th: 3.205; 4th: 3.909; O/D 3rd: 4.429; overdrive 3rd: 5.402; 2nd: 8.470; 1st: 13.446; reverse: 12.098:1

Not pristine, certainly, but typical of so many late-model UK-market MGBs, which used SU HIF4 carburettors. The direct-acting brake servo on this 1980 model had been standardized since May 1977.

NOTE: Overdrive became standard on home market cars from June 1975. From start of 1977 MY, first-gear internal ratio became 3.333/overall ratio 13.03:1.

BRAKES

Front, type	Lockheed disc, hydraulic
Front, size	10.75in diameter
Rear, type	Lockheed drum, hydraulic
Rear, size	10 × 1.75in
Servo	Lockheed

STEERING

Type	Rack and pinion
Turns (L-to-L)	2.9
Turning circle	32ft 6in (10m) approx. between kerbs

FRONT SUSPENSION

Type	Independent, coil springs, wishbones, on separate pressed-steel cross member
Anti-roll bar	None on Roadsters until June 1976, then standard once again; standard on GTs
Dampers	Lever arm, hydraulic

REAR SUSPENSION

Type	Beam axle, half-elliptic leaf springs
Anti-roll bar	None until 1976, standard with revised suspension from start of 1977 MY
Dampers	Lever arm, hydraulic

WHEELS AND TYRES

Wheel size	14in diameter, 4.5in Rostyle
Optional wire wheels	14in diameter, 4.5in rim width
Tyres	Radial-ply
Tyre size	165–14in

CAPACITIES

Engine oil	6.0 pints
Gearbox oil	5.0 pints
Gearbox + overdrive oil	6.0 pints
Rear axle oil	1.5 pints
Cooling system	10.0 pints
Fuel tank	12.7 Imperial gallons, 10.0 Imperial gallons for North American market

DIMENSIONS

Length	13ft 2.25in (4,019mm)
Width	4ft 11.7in (1,516mm)
Height (unladen)	4ft 2.9in (1,293mm)
Wheelbase	7ft 7in (2,311mm)
Front track	4ft 1in (1,245mm)
Rear track	4ft 1.25in (1,251mm)
Ground clearance	5in (127mm)
Weight (unladen):	Tourer 2,140lb (970kg)
	GT 2,260lb (1,025kg)

PERFORMANCE (UK models)

0–60mph (0–97kph)	12.2sec
Top speed	103mph (166km/h)
Standing ¼-mile	18.7sec
Overall fuel consumption	22mpg (13ltr/100km)
Typical fuel consumption	25mpg (11ltr/100km)

◆ In summer/autumn 1980 (though not officially revealed until January 1981, after the car had dropped out of production), a final run of LE cars were built. These consisted of: 421 Roadsters in Bronze Metallic and 580 GTs in Pewter Metallic.

RIVALS

The MGB, make no mistake, was the great survivor, for at a time when other companies were abandoning sports car sales, the MGB kept marching along. Of all the car's serious competition in the 1960s, only the Triumph TRs and Fiat 124 Spiders survived the 1970s.

Because the separate-chassis TR6 had only a short time to live when this type of MGB was launched, its influence was only peripheral. From 1975 to 1981, Triumph competition came from the Longbridge-styled TR7, although, amazingly, this new car never established superiority over the MGB (despite its being an obvious favourite among British Leyland bosses, with considerably more effort put behind its marketing).

More like the MGB than the TR6 had ever been – the TR7 had a four-cylinder engine, a solid rear axle and a monocoque structure – the TR7 was always a faster car than the MGB, with a softer ride, but even at first it cost more. In the spring of 1976, a UK-market MGB cost £2,400, while the newly launched TR7 cost £3,000.

The TR7 always suffered controversy because of its doubtful build-quality reputation and its fixed-head coupe style. Industrial action that hampered its production and two changes of assembly plant did not help, and the Roadster (convertible style) did not appear until 1979. The TR7 remained in production for a year after the MGB had been retired, but it never truly became the 'classic' that the MGB was, and remains.

The Fiat 124 Spider (though not the longer-wheelbase coupe, which was dropped in 1975) was always a serious competitor, especially in North America. When this variety of MGB went on sale, the 124 Spider had a 118bhp/1.8-litre engine (or 93bhp in North America). The Spider then progressed to 2-litres in 1978, after which it was *only* sold in North America. With 87bhp and a 102mph (164km/h) top speed, clearly it dealt more successfully with the latest exhaust emissions regulations, and its Pininfarina styling still looked good.

In the end (and with a 1982 change of title to Pininfarina, not Fiat), it actually outlived the MGB, lasting until 1985. More than 200,000 had been built, of which at least 170,000 went to North America. But how many do you see today?

'Black bumper' MGBs, built from late 1974 to 1980, had this massive rear bumper, and also rode 1.5 inches higher off the ground than previous MGBs. Rear 'fog guard' lamps were only fitted to MGB after June 1979, and then only to Home Market cars.

ABOVE: Although riding higher off the ground to meet North American crash test regulations, the late-model (this is a 1980) MGB was still a handsome car. This is an LE GT, painted in the Pewter Metallic which was unique to that model.

BELOW: This is a 1975 MGB GT, one of the early 'rubber bumper' models, showing how the big new front protection was blended into the little-changed panel work, and how the separate grille, as such, had been eliminated.

MGB MK II BLACK-BUMPER MODEL – 1974 TO 1980

TOP: To commemorate the end of the long run of MGBs, the company built 421 LE Roadsters in Bronze Metallic and 580 of these Pewter Metallic LE GTs. Among their special features were the special cast alloy wheels, the under-bumper front spoiler, and the special decals along the flanks.

BOTTOM: The striping behind the rear wheel arch of this 1980 model is special to the LE, but every other detail of this car is standard for late-model MGB GTs.

A detail, but an important one – the key slot and lift-up latch fitted to the boot lid of all MGBs over an 18-year period.

RIGHT: Rear lamp clusters of this type were fitted to all MGBs from 1969 onwards, and therefore to all 'rubber bumper' varieties.

BELOW: A smart roof-quarter badge for late-model GTs? Quite right, but there was a reason too. It was introduced from approximately March 1976, to hide a metal to metal seam which was no longer being lead-loaded before being painted.

MGB Mk II Black-Bumper Model – 1974 to 1980

ABOVE LEFT: Even though it was fashionable to delete swivelling front door quarter-lights by the 1970s (which tended to leak as seals and pivots wore out), they were used on each and every MGB, including all the 'rubber bumper' cars of 1974–80.

ABOVE RIGHT: The large black polyurethane bumper was there for a purpose – to get the MGB through the latest North American crash tests – but it was very carefully contoured to make it match the existing body panels. These had to be modified close to (and behind) the new bumpers, but their general profile was not changed.

BELOW: Over the years, several different types of door rear view mirrors were used on MGBs, but all 1974–80 MGBs used this variety as standard.

From the start-up of 1977 Model Year assembly, and coincident with the arrival of the new facia style, MGB seats were given what is often called the 'deck-chair' effect of fabric styling.

ABOVE: From June 1976, at the start of 1977 Model Year assembly, the UK Market MGB was given a completely new style of facia/instrument layout, where Triumph Spitfire instruments were used, and where there was a new four-spoke steering wheel (which was shared with North American market cars).

BELOW: When the much-modified facia/instrument style was introduced for the start-up of 1977 Model Year assembly, the MGB also benefitted from this useful central stowage locker.

RIGHT: This was the final type of RHD facia/instrument panel central display, as introduced from the start-up of 1977 Model Year assembly, and which carried on to the end, in October 1980.

CHAPTER FIVE

MGC

ALTHOUGH first thoughts on adding a larger-engined car to the MGB range came as early as 1960 (schemes involving a later-cancelled BMC V6 engine were drawn up), no serious design work started until 1961–62. For some time after this the problem was in deciding which type of straight-six cylinder engine should be used – and whether or not it could be persuaded to fit under the bonnet of the MGB shell.

Evolution was slow, and by no means purposeful. First, from 1963, BMC directed that the six-cylinder-engined car should be considered as a replacement for the Austin-Healey 3000, and that an Austin-Healey version of the new car should also be planned. Next, a major re-design of the existing C-Series engine took place, with the result that it was not until about 1965 that the design

began to settle down. At the insistence of Donald Healey, cancellation of an Austin-Healey derivative was not finalized until 1966; from then on, only the MGC version went ahead.

Then, as made clear earlier in Chapter 3, there was the need to standardize the structure and layout of the new six-cylinder-engined car with an updated MGB. This ensured that the MGC would use basically the same new all-synchromesh gearbox/overdrive installation, optional automatic transmission and final-drive arrangements as the MGB Mk II.

Aft of the bulkhead, the structure of the two cars would also be the same, but it was at the front end of the monocoque that the MGC would be unique – and therefore more costly to produce (this is described later). Except that the MGC used

Announced in 1967, but built for only two years, the MGC was built in Roadster (this style) or GT forms, and was strongly marketed in North America. The characteristic bonnet bulge is obvious from this aspect.

15in diameter road wheels, the only way to 'pick' an MGC was by noting that it had a big bonnet bulge to clear the lengthy six-cylinder engine and its forward-mounted cooling radiator. Apart from this, and the use of MGC badges on the tail, there were no other style differences, and the MGC was available with the same specification of Roadster or '2+2' GT body styles.

Announced in October 1967, the MGC went on sale immediately, and in spite of receiving a series of somewhat lukewarm press comments, began to sell steadily. A series of 'ifs' then ensured that it would remain in production for two years:

◆ *If* the press had liked it more, it might have sold better.

◆ *If* the structure/front suspension/ engine had not been so much more costly than those of the MGB, it might have made more profit for the company.

◆ *If* the new US exhaust emission regulations had not been so difficult to satisfy, the design team would have had more time to devote to it.

◆ *If* British Leyland had not been formed just after the MGC's birth, and the new and unsympathetic whizz-kid 'cost cutters' had not decided to kill off the MGC, it might have had a longer career.

Not even a 120mph (193km/h) top speed, and a significant mechanical improvement after only one year's production, could rise above that. In the end, only 9,002 MGCs were ever built.

STRUCTURE

Because the four-cylinder MGB's bulkhead and basic body panel profiles were to be retained for the MGC, it was never going to be easy to accommodate the much longer (and deeper) straight-six-cylinder engine.

Compared with the MGB, therefore, the MGC's monocoque had entirely different box-section chassis legs on each side of the longer engine and new inner wheel arch/engine bay valance pressings. A massive U-shaped front suspension/steering cross member was welded (not bolted) to the rest of the shell. This structure, of course, was the first and only MGB-related shell in which there had to be accommodation for the adjustment of the longitudinal torsion bars at their rear extremities, on a body structural member.

To provide space for the engine, not only was the MGB-type cooling radiator/cross member deleted – the radiator was mounted well forward – but the pressed aluminium bonnet panel was unique. The last few cars, incidentally, had a pressed-steel bonnet panel (this being the time when MGB Mk II production changed over in a similar manner). Not only was it necessary to add a wide and noticeable bulge towards the front, but there was also a single 'power bulge' above the forward SU carburettor as well.

Aft of the bulkhead, however, the new MGC structure was essentially the same as that of the MGB Mk II, coming complete with the wider and more squarer-sectioned transmission tunnel.

None of these necessary changes were ever adopted for the four-cylinder cars.

RUNNING GEAR

Although the engine of the MGC was a 2,912cc straight-six, with cast-iron cylinder block and head, plus twin SU carburettors, it was very different from the similar-sounding C-Series of the Austin-Healey 3000 which was just about to die off.

The new engine, the result of a redesign by BMC, had seven main crankshaft bearings, was about 2in (50mm) shorter than the old C-Series, and had been intended to be much lighter – but the saving was, in fact, only 44lb (20kg). Nor was it as powerful as the last of the Austin-Healey units (145bhp instead of 148bhp), the reduction mainly being due to friction from the extra bearings.

The same basic engine, incidentally, was also used in the Austin 3-litre saloon (ADO 61) of 1968–71, although it was never fitted to *any* other BMC or British Leyland car or light commercial vehicle.

It was a lazy-feeling engine, strangely reluctant to rev freely (a heavy flywheel had a lot to answer for), but it had a lot of mid-range torque. The MGC was marketed strongly in North America, but because this was merely the start of the exhaust emission limitation process, the only extra kit involved was the fitting of special inlet and exhaust manifolds (not adopted for R-o-W types), and a belt-driven air pump that injected air into the exhaust manifolds to encourage complete combustion at that point.

Amazingly, there was also a very limited production version, underbored and measuring 2,850cc, which was for use only in French market cars.

Benefiting from the big investment in a new all-synchromesh gearbox for the MGB, Austin 3-litre and some of BMC's light commercial vehicles, the MGC shared this design, although with a larger diaphragm-spring clutch (9.0in (23cm) diameter instead of 8.0in (20cm) diameter), which therefore dictated the use of a unique light-alloy casing.

Overdrive, like that of the MGB Mk II, the latest Laycock LH type, with a step-up ratio of 0.82:1, was always optional. It worked on top and third ratios.

Internal gearbox ratios take some sorting out – they differed between overdrive and non-overdrive cars, *and* (when axle ratios are taken into consideration) there were differences between 1968 and 1969 models too! The changeover occurred at chassis numbers 4236 (GTs) and 4266 (Roadsters).

Non-overdrive MGCs used identical internal ratios to the MGB Mk II, while all other MGCs used a unique set of internal ratios (the MGB GT V8 which followed was different yet again – *see* Chapter 6), which were in fact a closer-ratio set-up.

The MGC shared the same basic Salisbury rear axle type as all MGB Mk IIs, but with several different ratios:

◆ 3.071:1 on non-overdrive 1968 models.

◆ 3.307:1 on non-overdrive 1969 models and overdrive 1968 models, and all automatic transmission models.

◆ 3.70:1 on overdrive 1969 models.

Borg Warner Type 35 automatic transmission was an option on all MGCs, with three forward ratios, and (when specified) with the selector lever/quadrant on the transmission tunnel in the place of a conventional gear-change lever. Statistics show that (compared with the MGB) it was surprisingly popular – being fitted to 556 Roadsters and 764 GTs, a total of 1,320 cars, or 15 per cent of total production.

SUSPENSION, STEERING AND BRAKES

The easy way to summarize this is to point out that the MGC's rear suspension was identical to that of the MGB Mk II, while the front was completely different.

To deal with the extra bulk, weight and rather awkward positioning of the long six-cylinder engine, an entirely new type of front suspension was needed. First of all, the shape of the cross member was unique, being heavily bowed under the sump of the engine, and sweeping up at its extremities to provide pick-up points for the new front suspension itself.

Unlike the MGB, the MGC front suspension featured longitudinal torsion bars (Jaguar E-Type fashion), the rear ends of which were anchored to the bodyshell under the seats, and telescopic hydraulic dampers, with a reshaped and very firm anti-roll bar as standard.

Once again, for space reasons, the steering, which was still rack and pinion, differed in detail from that of the MGB. To keep down steering efforts, it was considerably lower-geared (3.5 turns lock-to-lock). The steering wheel itself had a sewn-on black leather rim cover.

Except for different spring and damper rates, the rear suspension layout was identical with that of the MGB GT Mk II.

Despite the fact that the wheels looked like those of the MGB Mk II – a choice of steel disc or centre-lock wires were available – they were of 15in rather than 14in diameter, both types having 5.0in rims. Radial-ply tyres of 165–15in were standard, this being a 'first' for MG.

Although the same basic type of disc front/drum rear brake installation was chosen, for the MGC

This is the standard colour and specification of an MGC engine, as fitted at Abingdon from 1967 to 1969. The 'flying saucer' above the inlet manifold was the positive crankcase breather valve – which was moved on later versions of this model.

alone (but never on the MGB) these were supplied by Girling, the front discs being larger (11.06in diameter), while the rear drums were smaller but wider (9 × 2.5in). Vacuum servo assistance was standard – North American market examples having twin servos, one for each individual front or rear circuit.

ELECTRICAL EQUIPMENT

Except where the unique engine was concerned, the MGC's electrical equipment was very similar to that of the MGB. On the engine itself, there was a Lucas 16AC (1969 models = 16ACR) alternator to provide electrical power and a Lucas M418G pre-engaged starter motor. Storage was by a pair of Lucas FG11E 11-plate, 6-volt batteries.

COCKPIT AND TRIM

There was little obvious difference in trim, carpeting, equipment and instrumentation between the MGC and the contemporary MGB Mk II – which was a bone of contention for MGC purchasers. Why, they asked, should they be required to pay so much more money for their cars when they *looked* the same as the MGB! However, if you look carefully, the speedometer was calibrated up to 140mph, while the rev-counter was red-lined at 5,500rpm.

As on MGB Mk IIs, there was a different style of facia for North American market cars (for the USA, right from the start; for Canada, from August 1968), while on Roadsters there was a choice

between a 'packaway' or 'foldaway' soft-top mechanism. A full tonneau cover was optional.

For the first year – the 1968 MY cars – the trim was nearly identical to all the first six-year generation of MGBs, and apart from the use of the leather-rimmed steering wheel it was effectively impossible to pick an MGC cabin from that of an MGB. All cars had full carpeting, the seats having contrast-colour piping to delineate trim panels. There was provision for a radio, but this was not standard.

Safety belts had to be fitted to all home market MGCs (although wearing them was not

The MGC had 15in wheels – these centre-lock wires were a factory option – which were 1in larger in diameter than those of the MGB.

OPTIONS

COLOURS

ON BOTH MODELS UNLESS NOTED:
- Sandy Beige (GT only)
- Black
- Mineral Blue

- Dark British Racing Green
- Grampian Grey (GT only)
- Tartan Red
- Old English White

- Snowberry White
- Pale Primrose Yellow
- Metallic Golden Beige
- Metallic Riviera Silver Blue

ACCESSORIES

MAJOR OPTIONS ONLY:
- Wire wheels
- Radio
- Heater/demister (standard for export)
- Fresh-air unit, as alternative to heater
- Hazard warning lights
- Rear compartment seat cushion

- Tonneau cover (Roadster)
- Heated rear window glass (GT)
- Folding soft-top mechanism
- Overdrive
- Automatic transmission
- Removable hardtop (Roadster)

DATES	October 1967–September 1969
CHASSIS NUMBERS	101–9102 (both Roadster and GT)
PRODUCTION BREAK POINTS	Oct. 1968–4266, start of 1969 MY (Roadster) Nov. 1968–4236, start of 1969 MY (GT)
TOTAL PRODUCED	4,544 Roadster 4,458 GT

compulsory until the late 1970s) – these were mostly of the Kangol 'static' (fixed-length) variety.

For the second Model Year (1969) – and as for the MGB Mk II at this time – a new seat, with different trim pattern style but without colour-contrasting piping, was adopted. At the same time, the seat frame was changed, and a degree of adjustable recline was built into the backrests, this being controlled by a chrome lever built into the side of the seat squab itself. There was still no between-seats centre console of any variety in MGBs of this period, and so the MGC did not have one either.

PRODUCTION

Throughout its short two-year life, the MGC was assembled at Abingdon, in the same historic buildings that had assembled every MG sports car since 1969. Taking over rapidly from the Austin-Healey 3000, it also assumed the assembly facilities of that car too. Although all major pressings were stamped at Pressed Steel, Swindon, complete bodyshells came from two sources:

◆ Roadster shells were jigged and welded together at the Morris Bodies Branch factory in Coventry, where they were also painted and trimmed, before being transported to Abingdon.

◆ GT shells were jigged and welded together at Swindon, then trucked to the Cowley body plant for painting and trimming, and finally transported to Abingdon.

As with every other MGB derivative, no major MGC component was manufactured at Abingdon. Engines – the 29G type that succeeded the original BMC C-Series power unit – were manufactured at the erstwhile 'Morris Engines Branch' factory in Coventry, while the gearboxes (which were very closely related to those of the MGB Mk II) were manufactured in the 'Tractors and Transmissions' factory in Birmingham. Many other MGB component suppliers – for wheels, tyres, electrics, instruments – were also chosen to supply pieces for the MGC.

CAREER

The MGC was only in series production for two years – from October 1967 to September 1969 – a period during which just over 9,000 cars were manufactured. Because only 240 MGCs were completed before the end of 1967, and because Austin-Healey 3000 assembly ended in December 1967, there was virtually no overlap between the old and new generations of straight-six-engined sports cars.

The MGC was officially launched in October 1967, and deliveries, slow at first, began almost at once. Most of the early cars were Roadsters, and almost all of them were for the UK market, but exports – particularly to North America – began in earnest during the winter.

Even at this stage in the MGB/C/B V8 range's history, it is fascinating to see how vital the North American market was to these cars. As far as the MGC was concerned, in a two-year life, 5,567 cars would be exported, of which no fewer than 4,256 (76 per cent) went to North America. There were no CKD deliveries, and only 163 right-hand-drive cars were originally exported.

Less than enthusiastic road tests did not help the cause of the MGC, yet it was not long before at least 100 MGCs were being produced every week. For the first Model Year – really from October 1967 to December 1968 – 4,128 MGCs were produced, these having the original combination of gear ratios and axle ratios that have already been described.

MGC

ENGINE

Layout	Six-cylinder, in-line
Block material	Cast iron
Head material	Cast iron
Peak power	145bhp (net) @ 5,250rpm
Peak torque	170lb ft @ 3,400rpm
Bore	83.34mm
Stroke	88.9mm
Cubic capacity	2,912cc
Compression ratio	9.0:1

FUEL SUPPLY

Carburettors	SU constant-vacuum
Type	2 × HS6
Fuel pump	SU electric

ELECTRICAL

Earth	Negative
Battery	2 × 58AH 6-volt
Generator	Lucas alternating-current alternator
Starter motor	M418G, Lucas, pre-engaged

MANUAL TRANSMISSION

Clutch	Single-plate, diaphragm spring
Clutch diameter	9.0in (23cm)
Gearbox type	Manual, four-speed, all synchromesh

Internal ratios

Non O/D, 1968 MY	4th: 1.00; 3rd: 1.382; 2nd: 2.167; 1st: 3.440; reverse: 3.095:1
O/D, 1968 MY, all cars 1969 MY	4th: 1.00; 3rd: 1.307; 2nd: 2.058; 1st: 2.98; reverse: 2.679:1

Overall gear ratios

Non O/D, 1968 MY	4th: 3.071; 3rd: 4.24; 2nd: 6.65; 1st: 10.56; reverse: 9.50:1
O/D, 1968 MY	O/D 4th: 2.71; 4th: 3.307; O/D 3rd: 3.544; 3rd: 4.32; 2nd: 6.80; 1st: 9.85; reverse: 8.86:1
Non O/D, 1969 MY	4th: 3.307; 3rd: 4.32; 2nd: 6.80; 1st: 9.85; reverse: 8.86:1
O/D, 1969 MY	O/D 4th: 3.034; 4th: 3.70; O/D 3rd: 3.965; 3rd: 4.836; 2nd: 7.615; 1st: 11.026; reverse: 9.912:1
Optional overdrive (and ratio)	Laycock LH-Type, 0.82:1

AUTOMATIC TRANSMISSION

Type	Borg Warner Type 35
	Three forward ratios, plus torque converter
Internal ratios	Top: 1.00; intermediate: 1.45; low: 2.39; reverse: 2.09:1
Overall ratios	Top: 3.307; intermediate: 4.795; low 7.903; reverse: 6.911:1

BRAKES

Front, type	Girling disc, hydraulic
Front, size	11.06in diameter
Rear, type	Girling drum, hydraulic
Rear, size	9 × 2.50in

STEERING

Type	Rack and pinion
Turns (L-to-L)	3.5
Turning circle	35ft 9in (11m) approx. between kerbs

FRONT SUSPENSION

Type	Independent, longitudinal torsion bar springs, wishbones
Anti-roll bar	Standard
Dampers	Telescopic, hydraulic

REAR SUSPENSION

Type	Beam axle, half-elliptic leaf springs
Anti-roll bar	None
Dampers	Lever arm, hydraulic

WHEELS AND TYRES

Wheel size	15in diameter, 5.0in rim width
Optional wire wheels	15in diameter, 5.0in rim width
Tyres	Radial-ply
Tyre size	165–15in

CAPACITIES

Engine oil	12.8 pints
Gearbox oil	5.0 pints
Gearbox + overdrive oil	6.3 pints
Rear axle oil	1.75 pints
Cooling system	18.5 pints
Fuel tank	12.0 Imperial gallons

DIMENSIONS

Length	12ft 9.23in (3,891mm)
Width	4ft 11.7in (1,516mm)
Height (unladen):	Tourer 4ft 2.25in (1,276mm)
	GT 4ft 3.0in (1,295mm)
Wheelbase	7ft 7in (2,311mm)
Front track	4ft 2in (1,270mm)
Rear track	4ft 1.25in (1,251mm)
Ground clearance (unladen)	4.5in (114mm)
Weight (unladen):	Tourer 2,460lb (1,116kg)
	GT 2,610lb (1,184kg)

PERFORMANCE

MANUAL ROADSTER [AUTOMATIC, GT]

0–60mph (0–97kph)	10.0sec [10.9sec]
Top speed	120mph (193km/h) [116mph (187km/h)]
Standing ¼-mile	17.7sec [18.2sec]
Overall fuel consumption	17.5mpg (16ltr/100km) [19.0mpg (15ltr/100km)]
Typical fuel consumption	19mpg (15ltr/100km) [20mpg (14ltr/100km)]

Visually, of course, there was little difference between the 1968 MY and 1969 MY models (one way to pick them, was to note the reclining seats in the later cars), but the later cars certainly had better acceleration and somehow felt better balanced. No fewer than 4,874 1969 MY cars were produced before the tap was turned off in September 1969 – however, it subsequently transpired around 150 cars had been built without orders, and MG's London distributors, University Motors, subsequently took them all over on favourable terms.

Automatic transmission was available throughout and proved to be very popular. No fewer than 1,320 automatic transmission cars – 556 of them Roadsters – were produced, the vast majority (937 cars) going to North America. Although there were signs that demand might pick-up, the combination of more impending US engine emissions regulations and the Leyland rush to 'rationalize' meant that the MGC was killed off before its time.

RIVALS

If the Austin-Healey 3000 had not died away just as the MGC was launched, it would have been an obvious in-house competitor, but as the MGC was developed to take over from that car, this never occurred.

Instead, from 1967 to 1969 the MGC competed, in a very narrow market sector, against Reliant's Scimitar GTE and Triumph's TR5/TR6. In Britain the Ford Capri 3000GT would not go on sale until the MGC had been discontinued, while in North America the Datsun 240Z did not get into showrooms until the last MGC had been sold.

In Europe, at first, it was the 150bhp/2.5-litre fuel-injected Triumph TR5, with its separate chassis frame, which was a head-on rival, although there was no GT or automatic version and the style was old. Even so, the TR5 had all-independent suspension and was priced at £1,261. From January 1969, the restyled TR6 offered a makeover around the same package.

In North America the MGC had an easier time against the Triumph, where the TR5 was a TR250, with only 105bhp and a lot less performance, this deficiency being carried forward with the TR6.

Reliant competition – in small but growing numbers (thirty cars a week was good for the Tamworth concern) – came from the Ford 3-litre/128bhp V6-engined Scimitar GT at first, then from late 1968 with the larger and more versatile hatchback GTE, though neither car was available as an open Roadster. Both were built on separate ladder-style chassis, with glass-fibre bodies, and were not as well detailed or built as the MGs. In 1968 Scimitar GTs cost £1,576 and in 1969 GTEs were £1,797, so the MG's price advantage was considerable.

ABOVE: The MGC was always fitted with 15in diameter wheels – perforated steel discs being standard, with this type of centre-lock wire-spoke wheels as optional extras.

BELOW: From the front, this Tartan Red MGC is easily identified by the wide bonnet bulge, accentuated by the transverse brightwork strip, which was needed to clear the forward-mounted cooling radiator.

TOP: How can we possibly tell that this is a six-cylinder MGC, and not the four-cylinder MGB? Only by spotting that this car has 15in, instead of 14in wheels, for the bonnet bulge cannot be seen from this angle.

ABOVE: Although the MGC had a much larger and more powerful engine than the MGB model from which it was developed, the two cars still looked almost identical. On the boot lid, however, are the important letters MGC. This Tartan Red car has wire-spoke wheels and a radio, both of which were extras.

ABOVE: The rear-end style of the MGC was identical with that of the MGB Mk II, which was launched at the same time.

LEFT: All MGCs were fitted with this original-style stop/tail/indicator lamp cluster, for the design was not changed until the model had been withdrawn from production.

BELOW: On the MGC, the only badge displayed was on the boot lid, immediately above the MG octagon. There was nothing on the nose of the car.

RIGHT: Along with the MGB Mk II, with which the interior trim and equipment was shared, on the door trims all MGCs were fitted with this pull-out door handle, along with a closing loop.

BELOW: The standard trim on all MGCs featured leather-faced seats with colour-contrasting piping.

OPPOSITE PAGE

TOP: Trim and decoration detail of a standard-equipment MGC included the bar down behind the centre of the screen, the swivelling quarter windows fixed to the doors, the push-button door handles and the remote locking barrels.

BOTTOM: This is the standard (in this case, well-matured, with much use having gone into those seats) of a 25-year-old MGC. Note the three sprung-spoke steering wheel, and the vertically-mounted, straight gear lever.

THIS PAGE

ABOVE: Like the MGB of the day, the MGC had a three-sprung spoke steering wheel as standard. The diameter was no less than 16.5 inches – this helped to reduce steering loads at low speeds – and the rim was covered with carefully stitched leather.

BELOW: Although the MGC's 2,912cc six-cylinder had identical bore/stroke/capacity dimensions to that of the old Austin-Healey 3000, this was an entirely different unit, with a seven-main-bearing crankshaft. The alternator and vertically-mounted oil filter body were both standard.

LEFT: The inlet manifold and carburettor of a standard-specification MGC looks like this. The carburettors were twin SU HS6 types.

BELOW: A Girling Mark 2B vacuum servo unit was standard equipment on all MGCs, for delivery to all markets.

BOTTOM: Although the heater on MGCs was standard on export-market cars (alternatively a fresh air unit could be specified), it was still an optional extra on UK-market cars until late 1968; nevertheless, almost all cars had them fitted.

CHAPTER SIX

MGB GT V8

1973 to 1976

HERE was a good and logical idea that never succeeded as hoped. Before the formation of British Leyland, the only way to up-engine an MGB had been to choose a BMC straight-six, but thereafter there was a theoretical choice of the 3.5-litre light-alloy Rover V8 or the 3-litre overhead-camshaft Triumph Stag too.

Even so, there was no project work on an MGC successor at Abingdon until 1971, although an enterprising engineer, Ken Costello, had started selling Rover V8-engined conversions of MGBs, which gained rave reviews in the motoring press.

British Leyland reacted by challenging Abingdon's engineers to do a better job, which they did, very rapidly. No one, however, could warm to the idea of using a Stag V8 engine (not solely because

of marque jealousy, but also due to the Stag engine's poor reputation), and as British Leyland was already promoting the wider use of the Rover V8 engine, the choice made itself.

This was always going to be a speedy, low-budget programme, which explains why the GT V8 ended up as a minimum-change model. The first-ever prototype took to the road in September 1971, the first pre-production cars were assembled in December 1972–January 1973, and the new car was finally revealed to the public in August 1973.

Intriguingly, this model was only ever built as a GT coupe (no Roadster, not even test cars, were ever built), and was only ever sold on the UK market. By MGB standards it was extremely well specified, with every normal 'extra' – such as overdrive

The MGB GT V8, built from 1973 to 1976, was the fastest and most refined of all this Abingdon-built family. Early examples had the chrome-bumper style, but black-bumper cars like this Damask Red type were in production from late 1974 until the end.

– catalogued as standard equipment. In character this was definitely more 'GT' than 'sports car', yet until the 'retro' RV8 arrived in 1993 it was the fastest MG ever put on sale.

Why no Roadster? No clear answer here, except that this was a Product Planning-led programme that emphasized the luxurious nature of the car. There have also been unconfirmed stories of a reluctance by MG engineers to put so much torque (193lb ft – nearly twice that of the four-cylinder cars) through a Roadster shell.

Selling the car only on the UK market was said to be due to the limited number of Range Rover-based engines that could be allocated, and to the fact that to sell the car in North America it would have been extremely costly to re-engineer the car as a unique model to meet every exhaust emission and safety regulation.

Even so, British Leyland was confident enough to set up a dedicated assembly line for the GT V8 at Abingdon. They must have been disappointed that initial demand soon fell away, for by 1976 there was no doubt that many more V8 engines could have been supplied from Rover if they had been needed.

This derivative was in series production for almost exactly three years. Of the 2,591 cars eventually produced, 1,926 were of the original 'chrome bumper' variety, followed by just 665 'black bumper' derivatives.

STRUCTURE

Remember, straight away, that the V8-engined car was only made in a GT version – even though many MGB enthusiasts later produced their own 'private-enterprise' cars in the Roadster shell.

Although the Rover V8 engine was bulky, the existing structure could almost, but not quite, accommodate it without major changes being necessary. No bodyshell changes were needed aft of the bulkhead, or in the floor, but several pressings in and around the engine bay needed modification. Inner wheel arches (some call these engine bay valances) had to be reshaped to accommodate the wider engine and its exhaust manifolds, and there were local dimples close to those manifolds.

At the same time, the 'chassis legs' which ran back from the front suspension cross member were also reshaped, not least because the clutch bell-housing was larger than before. Toeboard panels in the bulkhead were slightly reshaped, and for carburettor clearance purposes very minor changes were made to the side-on profile of the bonnet pressing (this change being shared with four-cylinder MGBs).

Since the same size and shape of four-speed, all-synchromesh gearbox, overdrive and rear axle as the four-cylinder cars were being employed, no changes were needed to the rest of the shell, and many of the pressings and fittings were common with the four-cylinder cars.

When the time came for the 'black bumper' style to be incorporated at the end of 1974, the shell of the GT V8 was modified in the same way (already described) as the 1975-model four-cylinder MGB.

RUNNING GEAR

Basically (although it was not quite as simple as this), the GT V8 was a re-engined MGB GT, with the same structure and style, the same basic transmission and the same rear axle:

◆ The Rover-manufactured 3,528cc V8 was a modified version of the low-compression (8.25:1) Range Rover power unit, which had a cast aluminium cylinder block and cylinder heads, plus hydraulic tappets. For installation reasons (there was space, but not that much space under the MGB bonnet), there were unique cast exhaust manifolds and secondary inlet manifold, which placed the twin SU carburettors at the rear of the engine, rather than centrally. An oil filter and oil cooler were both remotely mounted, ahead of the engine itself.

For the GT V8, this engine was rated at 137bhp at 5,000rpm, and it is

Door mirrors of this squared-up pattern were standard on MGB GT V8s.

worth noting that, at this time, Range Rover engines were rated at 130bhp at 5,000rpm, while the high-compression unit in the Rover 3500S produced 143bhp at 5,000rpm. The decision to use a less than optimum engine in a sporting MG has never been explained, but even so the GT V8 had a top speed of 125mph (200km/h).

- The transmission needed a unique casting to envelop the larger diaphragm spring clutch, which was of 9.5in (24cm) diameter, while yet another unique set of internal gearbox ratios were developed. Internal first gear ratio, incidentally, was raised from 3.138:1 to 3.036:1 when the 'rubber bumper' specification was introduced.

- Overdrive, the Laycock LH type, was standard, but operated only on top gear (overdrive was not standardized on every RHD four-cylinder MGB until June 1976, and was never standard on North American models).

- The final drive ratio was 3.071:1 in a Salisbury-type casing – an existing CWP set, in fact the same as on 1968-model non-overdrive MGCs. This high ratio, of course, was never used on four-cylinder MGBs.

SUSPENSION, STEERING AND BRAKES

Unlike the MGC, which had featured a unique front-end, the suspension of the GT V8 was closely based on that of the four-cylinder cars of the period, but with many detail changes.

To ensure adequate ground clearance under the V8's sump, the front cross member was modified to slightly raise the car, while the front coil springs were longer, and the rear leaf springs were slightly realigned. Front and rear springs were both slightly stiffer than those of the four-cylinder cars, and there were new, non-crushable lower-wishbone bush mountings.

From the start-up of 'rubber bumper' production, all these layout and ground-clearance changes were commonized with the four-cylinder cars.

The rack and pinion steering gear was very similar to that fitted to four-cylinder MGBs of the period, and although there was a unique type of steering column lock and upper column shroud/switchgear layout, the alloy three-spoked steering wheel was also the same.

The GT V8, at least, had unique Dunlop 14in road wheels with 5in rims, these featuring cast alloy perforated centres, to which chrome-plated steel rims were riveted. Just to confuse the issue, though, the same wheels, repainted, were to be fitted on the 'Jubilee' four-cylinder MGB GTs of 1975!

This was also the first MGB to have tubeless tyres, those being 175HR-14in radials from Goodyear, Michelin or Pirelli (fitted, at least, in matching car sets).

Although the front discs were considerably thicker than on the four-cylinder cars, and a brake servo was standard equipment, the Lockheed installation was based on that of the four-cylinder cars.

ELECTRICAL EQUIPMENT

Like other four-cylinder MGBs of the period, the GT V8 was built up around a Negative Earth installation, but the use of a Rover-manufactured V8 engine meant that quite a lot of the electrical equipment had to be revised.

Early cars still had two 6-volt batteries, but soon after launch (at Chassis No. 604) a change was made to a single 12-volt battery – the same move that was being made with the four-cylinder MGBs. The V8 engine actually used an AC Delco alternator (Lucas was apparently not best pleased …), and a Lucas 3M100 starter motor was included.

COCKPIT AND TRIM

For all the obvious ease of production reasons, the trim and interior equipment of the GT V8 were very like that of the mid-1970s four-cylinder cars. Even the choice of body colours and trim colours were the same. Because this car was to be sold on the UK market only, there was only one set of instruments and fittings to be accommodated. (In view of the car's high price this, some critics pointed out, could not really be justified.)

The V8 car, however, had seat headrests as standard and inertia-reel safety belts were also standard (they became standard on four-cylinder cars soon afterwards). The steering column control stalk arrangement was different from the four-cylinder cars – the multi-function left stalk, pointing towards the centre of the car, also operated the overdrive switch. Because these new stalks required a bigger shroud to accommodate them, the instruments (including a 140mph speedometer – there was no kph alternative, of course) were of a smaller, 80mm, diameter. (Four-cylinder cars did not adopt the GT V8 instruments and column controls until the rubber bumper variety of cars arrived late in 1974.)

The steering wheel was the same as that used on four-cylinder MGBs of the period.

PRODUCTION

As with contemporary four-cylinder MGBs, GT V8 production, at Abingdon, was a 100 per cent assembly process, for no component of any consequence was manufactured at the little MG factory.

In this 1973–76 period, as with the four-cylinder cars, all the GT V8 bodyshells were pressed and assembled by Pressed Steel Fisher at Swindon, before being trucked to the Cowley body plant complex for lead-loading, then for painting and trimming, before then being transported to Abingdon for final assembly.

Although all the running gear was then trucked in, in the four-cylinder manner, this time some supplies came from different sources. V8 engines were manufactured at the Rover factory at Acocks Green (near Solihull) in the West Midlands, and because the gearbox was closely related to that of the current MGB, it was manufactured on the same facilities in the Birmingham area. The back axle, sharing its ratio with one of those employed in the MGC, was also a modified MGB/MGC item.

Abingdon assembly took place in the same way as all other MGB derivatives, although for a time the GT V8 had its own dedicated assembly line. As ever, this process included setting up the partly finished cars on three levels – originally on the 'Trim Deck', then on the 'Elevated Line' where all underbody pieces were added, and finally, when the wheels had been fixed into place, on the final section of the line. In all cases it was 'Abingdon-power' (i.e. the workforce!) which moved the cars from one station to the next.

CAREER

The GT V8 was only in full production for three years – effectively from May 1973 until May 1976, though pre-production cars at the start plus stragglers at the finish stretched this a little. Public launch came in mid-August 1973, by which time at least 400 cars had already been assembled at Abingdon.

British Leyland spokesmen always maintained that the limited production was due to a shortage of V8 engines from Rover, but this was only partly true. Other reasons were that the GT V8 was only ever sold in the UK, and after the Energy Crisis of 1973–74 it was always going to be difficult to sell large-engined cars of this type. (To give an idea of the relative volumes of engine users, in 1973 at least 20,000 Rover-badged V8-engined cars were assembled.)

No fewer than 1,070 of the 2,591 cars were produced in calendar year 1973, effectively in seven months, with the peak monthly figure of 176 cars

No chance of missing the GT V8's Chassis Number – at 002147, this places this particular car as a late-1974 built machine, soon after the 'rubber bumper' style was introduced.

MGB GT V8

PRODUCTION	
DATES	April 1973–September 1976
CHASSIS NUMBERS	G/D2D1 101–2903
PRODUCTION BREAK POINTS	October 1974–introduction of polyurethane-bumpered models at Chassis No. 2101
TOTAL PRODUCED	2,591 cars, all for the home market

being achieved in October. Production dropped to 853 cars in 1974, alarmingly so after August, but this was really to make way for the urgent introduction and build-up of polyurethane-bumpered four-cylinder MGBs, which were more urgently needed in the North American market 'pipeline'.

As with the four-cylinder cars, when the black bumper style was phased in, a new and different range of colours also became available.

Only 482 cars were assembled in 1975, and a mere 183 followed in 1976. The last car of all, carrying Chassis No. 2903, was produced on 10 September 1976.

Chrome-bumpered cars totalled 1,856 examples, with 735 'black-bumpered' examples built in 1974–76.

During this time, the V8-engined car was only produced as a GT coupe, and all cars had manual-plus-overdrive transmission, although in later years many MG enthusiasts applied the same type of running gear to convert their MGB Roadsters into V8 Roadsters.

Just one 'Anniversary Special' GT V8 was produced, in 1975 – like the equivalent four-cylinder cars, this had a British Racing Green-plus-gold striping colour scheme.

RIVALS

Because the GT V8 was only ever sold in the UK, it is simple enough to pinpoint its rivals in the marketplace. Let us not forget, this car was less of a sports car than a GT machine, for there was no 'open to the elements' character and a great deal of understated refinement.

A trawl through the price lists of 1973 turns up a very short list of rivals – closed cars, that is, which offered the same level of performance,

engine refinement and comfort. Only three of them – the Ford Capri 3000GXL, the Reliant Scimitar GTE and the Triumph Stag – were significant, and all of them were available with automatic transmission as an option.

The 136bhp/3-litre Capri, at £1,824, was a formidable competitor. Uncouth maybe, and forever tainted with the 'Essex Medallion Man' image, it was fast, durable, inexpensive to insure (at saloon-car rates) and cheap to maintain. In 1973 it had a 2+2 cabin, and from 1974 would be restyled with a larger cabin and a hatchback to match the MG. Backed by Ford's formidable marketing machine, it always outsold the GT V8.

Although the Reliant Scimitar GTE did not have the same sporting pedigree as the MG, it had already built up its own reputation since 1968. Powered by the same engine as the Capri, it had a separate chassis, was a near-120mph (193km/h) machine with a good-sized 2+2 cabin and a glass hatchback. Only the use of a glass-fibre bodyshell and doubtful build quality made it less than a head-on competitor at £2,480.

The V8-engined 3-litre Triumph Stag was, at once, a competitor and a Leyland family relative of the GT V8, although it shared no common parts, was built in another factory, and was sold through a different dealer chain.

If it had been more reliable and better built, the Stag would have been great competition for the GT V8, for it had an excellently trimmed cabin, equally as much space inside, and was also available as a soft-top. But the suspension (derived from the 2000 saloon) was over-soft, and the engine soon got a bad reputation. It would fade away a year after the GT V8 had been retired.

Other cars offered a similar package – the BMW 3.0CSi and Citroën SM among them – but their high prices put them in a separate universe.

MGB GT V8

ENGINE

Layout	Eight-cylinders, in 90-deg vee
Block material	Cast aluminium
Head material	Cast aluminium
Peak power	137bhp (net) @ 5,000rpm
Peak torque	193lb ft @ 2,900rpm
Bore	88.9mm
Stroke	71.1mm
Cubic capacity	3,528cc
Compression ratio	8.25:1

FUEL SUPPLY

Carburettors	SU constant-vacuum
Type	2 × HIF6
Fuel pump	SU electric

ELECTRICAL

Earth	Negative
Battery	
Chrome bumper cars	Two 6-volt
Polyurethane bumper cars	One 12-volt
Generator	AC Delco alternating-current alternator
Starter motor	3M100, Lucas, pre-engaged

MANUAL TRANSMISSION

Clutch	Single-plate, diaphragm spring
Clutch diameter	9.5in (24cm)
Gearbox type	Manual, four-speed, all-synchromesh
Internal ratios	O/D 4th: 0.82; 4th: 1.00; 3rd: 1.259; 2nd: 1.974; 1st: 3.138; reverse: 2.819:1
Overall ratios	O/D 4th: 2.518; 4th: 3.071; 3rd: 3.866; 2nd: 6.062; 1st: 9.637; reverse: 8.657:1
Overdrive (and ratio)	Laycock LH-Type, 0.82:1

BRAKES

Front, type	Lockheed disc, hydraulic
Front, size	10.7in diameter
Rear, type	Lockheed drum, hydraulic
Rear, size	10 × 1.7in
Servo assistance:	Lockheed, vacuum

STEERING

Type	Rack and pinion
Turns (L-to-L)	2.9
Turning circle	33ft 0in (10m) approx. between kerbs

FRONT SUSPENSION

Type	Independent, coil springs, wishbones
Anti-roll bar	Standard
Dampers	Lever arm, hydraulic

REAR SUSPENSION

Type	Beam axle, half-elliptic leaf springs
Anti-roll bar	None
Dampers	Lever arm, hydraulic

WHEELS AND TYRES

Wheel size	14in diameter, 5.0in rim width
Tyres	Radial-ply
Tyre size	175HR14in

CAPACITIES

Engine oil	9.0 pints
Gearbox + overdrive oil	6.3 pints
Rear axle oil	1.75 pints
Cooling system	16 pints
Fuel tank	12.0 Imperial gallons

DIMENSIONS

Length	
Chrome bumper cars	12ft 10.7in (3,929mm)
Polyurethane bumper cars	13ft 2.25in (4,020mm)
Width	5ft 0in (1,524mm)
Height (unladen)	4ft 2.0in (1,270mm)
Wheelbase	7ft 7in (2,311mm)
Front track	4ft 1in (1,244mm)
Rear track	4ft 1.25in (1,251mm)
Ground clearance (unladen)	4.5in (114mm)
Weight (unladen)	2,442lb (1,108kg)

PERFORMANCE

MANUAL (OVERDRIVE AS STANDARD) GT

0–60mph (0–97kph)	8.6sec
Top speed	124mph (200km/h)
Standing ¼-mile	16.4sec
Overall fuel consumption	23.4mpg (12ltr/100km)
Typical fuel consumption	25mpg (11ltr/100km)

The 'black bumper' style suited the late-model MGB GT V8 particularly well, especially when the car was painted in Damask Red.

TOP: Visually, this late-model MGB GT V8 looks absolutely original – except, that is, for the accessory fabric sunroof which was fitted after delivery.

BOTTOM: Not only was the MGB GT V8 a very fast and refined sports coupe, but a very practical one too – and was able to swallow a great deal of luggage through the lift-up hatchback.

TOP: To identify the MGB GT V8, MG fitted special cast alloy road wheels, and there was this V8 badge on the lift-up hatchback.

BOTTOM: Like all MGB GTs, the stowage area behind the seats of the GT V8 was well-trimmed, flat, and amazingly versatile – it could swallow cases, pushchairs, golf clubs, the lot.

LEFT: This 'MG BGT' badge was fitted to the hatchback lid of all MGB GT V8s.

BELOW RIGHT: British Leyland was proud of its ownership of MG in the 1970s, so MGB GT V8s were badged, on the near-side front wing, with a V8 and a British Leyland 'spiral' badge.

BOTTOM RIGHT: From early 1976 (and to cover up an un-lead-loaded panel joint) the GT V8 carried such a 'GT' badge on the top rear corner of the roof panel, just outboard of the hatchback aperture.

LEFT: These stop/tail-indicator rear lamp clusters had been introduced for all MGBs built from the start of 1970 Model Year, and were always fitted to GT V8s.

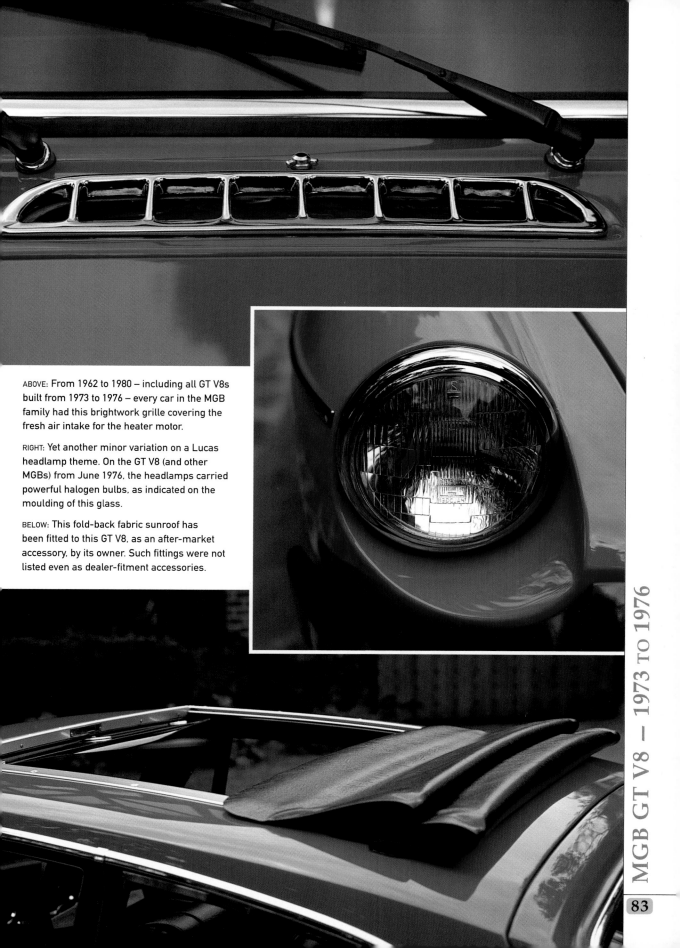

ABOVE: From 1962 to 1980 – including all GT V8s built from 1973 to 1976 – every car in the MGB family had this brightwork grille covering the fresh air intake for the heater motor.

RIGHT: Yet another minor variation on a Lucas headlamp theme. On the GT V8 (and other MGBs) from June 1976, the headlamps carried powerful halogen bulbs, as indicated on the moulding of this glass.

BELOW: This fold-back fabric sunroof has been fitted to this GT V8, as an after-market accessory, by its owner. Such fittings were not listed even as dealer-fitment accessories.

ABOVE: This style of alloy-spoked steering wheel was fitted to all MGB GT V8s. Although the facia/instrument/control layout looks familiar, for the GT V8 there was new column switchgear, and smaller-diameter instruments. The speedometer read up to 140mph.

BELOW: This was the layout of the MGB GT V8's centre console, but the radio was not a standard (or even an optional) item – it has been added, in the location provided – by the owner.

TOP: Black crackle finish, an MG badge ahead of the passenger's eyes, and a lockable glovebox were all standard equipment for the MGB GT V8.

ABOVE: On the GT V8, face-level ventilation grilles and the heater controls were all grouped together in the centre of the facia panel.

RIGHT: Like all post-1967 MGB-family types, this type of pull-out door handle, and the loop under it, were standard on MGB GT V8s. The hardware was shared with other BMC saloon cars of the period.

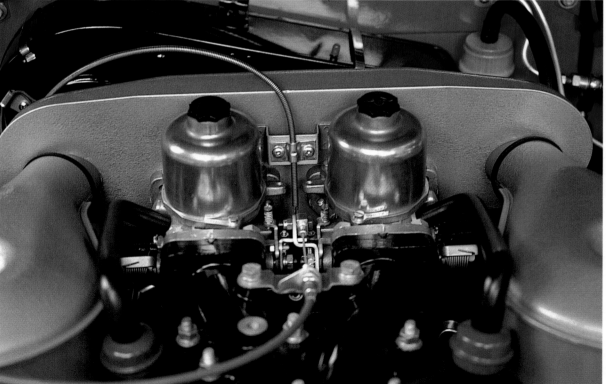

TOP: The big Rover-sourced V8 was packaged neatly under the bonnet of the MGB GT V8, with unique manifolding which featured the relocation of twin SU carburettors towards the passenger bulkhead.

BOTTOM: Twin SU HIF6 carburettors, mounted side by side, provided fuel-air mixture to the 3.5-litre V8 engine of the GT V8.

RIGHT: Eight cylinders meant eight HT ignition leads from a massive distributor on the MGB GT V8.

BELOW: The Rover-sourced engine of the GT V8 used an AC Delco alternator. Every other type of MG used a Lucas generator.

BOTTOM: Front-end engine bay detail shows that there was a neat protective mesh above the thermostatically-controlled cooling fan of the MGB GT V8.

THIS PLUG MUST NOT BE REMOVED WHEN ENGINE IS HOT

ABOVE: Fresh air for the SU carburettors of the GT V8 engine was drawn in through these manifolds, which drew air over the hot exhaust manifolds on the outside of the cylinder bank.

BELOW LEFT: The oil filter for the GT V8's engine was remotely mounted, at the right front of the engine bay, close to the cooling radiator.

BELOW RIGHT: The brake servo on the MGB GT V8 was standard equipment, a remotely-positioned Lockheed vacuum type mounted on the left side of the car, on the inner wheelarch.

Epilogue

COULD the MGB have been replaced? Should it have been replaced? Enthusiasts will always tell you that there should have been a new-generation car, but once British Leyland got its claws into MG and Abingdon, that possibility soon faded away.

When MG was an important part of BMC, top management usually smiled fondly on it, but once Leyland (which favoured Triumph) took control at Longbridge, that emotion soon faded away. Years before the MGB's career eventually came to an end, it was clear that there would be no successor – at least, not with an MG badge and not built at Abingdon. The miracle was that it kept on selling for as long as it did.

Even so, as an on-going classic and one whose reputation was secure, the MGB might have lasted even longer if it had not been badly hampered by the state and development of the North American market.

Once the Clean Air Act had been enacted in the USA, and the parallel tidal wave of safety and crash-test legislation had swept in, the cost of keeping current models abreast of the new regulations was colossal. British Leyland and the MG design team soon found that the majority of their technical resources had to go into meeting these, rather than in pressing ahead with new models.

Even so, there was a concerted effort to rectify the progressive throttling of the noble old B-Series engine, by substituting the modern 2-litre overhead-camshaft British Leyland O-Series power unit. This would have transformed the car's performance, with 127bhp instead of 95bhp for UK market cars and 95bhp instead of 67bhp for the North American market versions. For sale in Europe, there was even the possibility of producing a turbocharged version. All in all, in 1978 it looked as if the life of the MGB could be pushed on until 1984 at least.

For use in Austin-Morris family cars, this engine went into quantity production in 1978, although suitably-engined MGB prototypes had been constructed as early as 1975 and were always in evidence at Abingdon until the end came in 1980.

Throughout the 1970s, however, other priorities meant that the existing MGB model, whose style basically dated from 1962, could not be significantly changed. If they were looking for a new MG sports car in the mid and late 1970s, MGB enthusiasts were faced with buying a car that looked, sounded and felt much the same as it had always done.

One result was that some of these customers began to look elsewhere, which unfortunately meant that in the late 1980s sales gradually ebbed away. The fact that Abingdon production held up remarkably well is somewhat confusing, for stocks of unsold cars gradually built up in North America to unbalance the situation, this being one important factor in the number-crunchers' calculations.

MG's EX234 project was developed in the mid-1960s. It had all-independent Hydrolastic suspension, and was to have been built with a 1,275cc or a 1,798cc engine. Styling was by Pininfarina. One prototype was completed, but by 1966 it had to be put aside; it survives to this day.

The ADO21 project, conceived in 1969–70, never progressed beyond this clay styling mock-up stage. Styled at Longbridge, it was to have a transverse mid-engined/rear-drive layout, using the elements of the overhead camshaft 4-cylinder 1.75-litre Austin Maxi or 6-cylinder 2.2-litre Princess engine/transmission power packs. Many technical drawings were completed, but no running prototype was ever built.

The last MGB of all, therefore, was produced at Abingdon on 23 October 1980, after which cars were no longer built on that famous site.

WHAT MIGHT HAVE BEEN

Although it was on 10 September 1979 that British Leyland had announced that MG sports car assembly would cease in 1980, several attempts were made to stave off that evil day. The most important came from a consortium of businessmen headed by Alan Curtis and Peter Sprague (who had both been instrumental in pulling Aston Martin back from the brink in 1975), along with David Wickens (of British Car Auctions, who would became an important figure at Lotus in the early 1980s).

BL, it has to be said, took a more pragmatic view of the engineering and legislative problems than did the consortium. Freelance stylist William Towns was hired to produce facelift schemes – one such car was produced as a gesture of good intent – but although a provisional deal was made public on 31 March 1980, by mid-summer it had all collapsed when the consortium's funds could not be assembled.

And that, in Abingdon's terms, was that.

BRITISH MOTOR HERITAGE

In the 1980s, however, the British Motor Industry Heritage Trust further developed the business of sourcing parts for out-of-production British Leyland models. Led by the expertise of David Bishop, British Motor Heritage, a dedicated subsidiary company, located all the press tools for the MGB body shell, re-hired redundant staff both from Pressed Steel and the MG Abingdon factory, set up new premises in Faringdon, close to Abingdon – and from 1988 began re-manufacturing complete MGB shells!

Except for a period when this little factory's output had to concentrate on producing shells for the RV8 model – see below – the MGB shell has been in production ever since, with sales now well into the thousands. To cope with this, and the assembly of other shells, a move to larger premises soon followed.

Complete bodyshells for four-cylinder MGBs – whether Roadster or GT, whether 'chrome bumper' or 'black bumper' types – were all made available, and as the twenty-first century opened they were still being made to order. Except that they were not quite 'as original' – for example, bonnet pressings were in steel instead of aluminium – they were totally authentic. In 2001, a fully dressed Roadster shell cost approximately £3,000, a GT shell £3,500.

As an aside, one complication of the fact that BMW took control of the Rover group in 1994 (which controlled the BMIHT), then sold it off, piecemeal, in 2000, was that from that date BMW of Germany continued to be the legal owners of the British Motor Heritage concern (which continued to manufacture MGB bodyshells), but the BMH was no longer connected with the Heritage Trust, which kept all of MG's production records.

MG RV8 – A 1990s PHENOMENON

Although the MG brand died in 1980, this was only temporary, for under Austin-Rover it was revived from 1982 on a series of warmed-over Austin Metros, Maestros and Montegos. Throughout the

1980s, however, there was no sign of a revival of MG as a sports car.

Then, in 1989 (this was a period, incidentally, when British Aerospace was controlling the Rover Group) thoughts turned to reviving the sports cars. To produce an all-new model would take years, so as a holding measure consideration was given to reintroducing the MGB in one form or another as a short-term 'retro' model. Rover Special Products was set up for this purpose, as well as for developing other specialized Rover Group models.

After a number of other initiatives had been studied, 'Project Adder' took shape around the basis of the BMH-remanufactured MGB bodyshell. After a great deal of work had gone into restyling the outer contours of the car, a new MG called the RV8 was unveiled in October 1992. Assembly in a dedicated facility at Cowley (in a re-equipped section of the old Pressed Steel factory) started early in 1993.

It is difficult to reduce the theme of the RV8 to a few words, for although there were elements of MGB GT V8 in it, this was a Roadster and almost every aspect of the car was different. In basic terms, the RV8 – of which, incidentally, only 2,000 would be built by 1995 and many of which were sold in Japan – was an MGB Roadster with an updated version of the V8's engine, but much more was involved than this. Think of an MGB, then stir in the following developments:

◆ Although the basic MGB Roadster bodyshell was retained, the style looked very different, for there were flared front and rear wheel arches, a bulged bonnet (to clear the V8 engine), new body-colour plastic bumpers, new style headlamp recesses and prominent under-door sills linking the front and rear outer wing panels.

◆ The interior was completely restyled, with a wooden facia/instrument board, plushy seats and a thick-rimmed, three-spoke, steering wheel. The doors no longer had fixed quarter-windows, and were equipped with body-colour exterior mirrors.

◆ The engine was a distant relative of that once used in the MGB GT V8, being a 3,946cc derivative, equipped with electronic fuel injection, and producing a beefy 190bhp. Naturally there were catalysts in the exhaust system, and the engine was backed by a five-speed all-synchromesh gearbox of the type previously used in Rover SD1 hatchbacks (though by this time, this Land Rover-built component was being supplied to companies like TVR and Morgan).

◆ Within the limits of space and investment, the chassis was retouched, the front and rear tracks were both widened, the front suspension was by double wishbones and telescopic dampers (no lever arms, in other words); telescopic dampers were also fitted at the rear, and there was a Quaife limited-slip differential in the rear axle.

◆ Inside the cockpit, squashy leather seats and door trims were standard, there was wall-to-wall wood on the facia panel, while the steering wheel and much of the switch gear came from the current Rover 800 model.

In many ways the RV8 was completely different from the four-cylinder MGB, and very different from the MGB GT V8 (with which it shared the same basic V8 engine), and its UK sales appeal was limited by a £25,440 basic price. Road tests showed that it could reach 136mph (220km/h), with 0–100mph in 18.5 seconds.

Unhappily, its ride and general appeal had not kept up with the ever-moving standards of the day, so it did not perhaps sell as well as Rover had hoped. UK sales were restricted, most RV8s were delivered to Japan, and it disappeared from the price lists in 1995.

MG'S REBIRTH

Although the Abingdon factory had been flattened, then redeveloped, in the 1990s, MG's sports car heritage lived on, though it took many years for a new model to be developed.

In the early 1990s, a new project got under way, Rover's new owners, BMW, approved of it, and the MGF was introduced in 1995, with bodyshells made by Mayflower in Coventry and final assembly located at the Longbridge factory.

This was made possible by the body structure suppliers, Mayflower, taking a financial stake in the investment, and also a slice of profits.

Except that it carried the famous badge, there was no direct connection between the MGF and the MGB, and naturally no components were shared. Although the MGF had a two-seater steel monocoque structure, it used a 16-valve 2-ohc 1.8-litre Rover K-Series engine which, together with a five-speed transmission, was mounted transversely behind the seats, driving the rear wheels.

The development of that car is an entirely different story ....

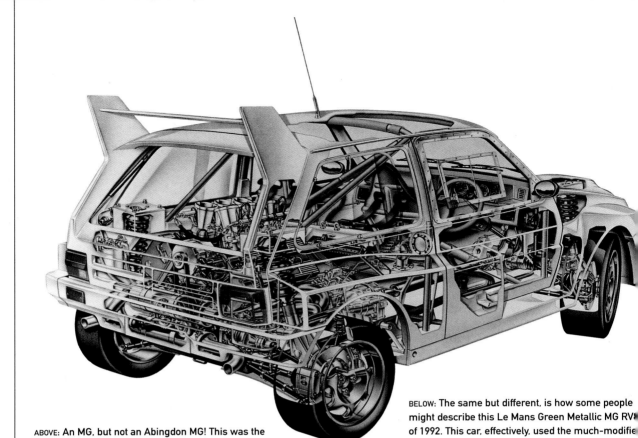

ABOVE: An MG, but not an Abingdon MG! This was the Metro 6R4, complete with mid/rear-mounted 3.0-litre V6 engine and four-wheel-drive, of which 200 were completed in 1985, and which was a promising rally car in 1986 before the World Championship rally programme was killed off.

BELOW: The same but different, is how some people might describe this Le Mans Green Metallic MG RV8 of 1992. This car, effectively, used the much-modified structure of an MGB, but with flared arches, different bumpers and prominent sills, with a 3.9-litre Rover V8 engine under the bonnet. 2,000 were sold before production ended in 1995.

ABOVE: A fascinating comparison between a 1960s-type MGB (right) and a 1992 MG RV8 (left). Clearly the two cars share the same monocoque, but the RV8 was different in so many ways.

BELOW: Using the MGB monocoque as the basis for a new 'retro' model, Rover developed the RV8, in which almost every external panel, plus the windscreen, bumpers and wheels, were updated for the 1990s. This car, of course, was not exported to North America, which partly explains the different shape and style of the bumpers from the late 1970s MGB.

THIS PAGE

TOP: For the RV8, there was a completely new interior style, including squashy seats, a full-width wooden facia panel, and a three-spoke steering wheel.

ABOVE: From the rear aspect, the link between the RV8 (this car) and the original MGB is clear, though the flared wheelarches, different tail lamp clusters, and different bumpers are obvious.

OPPOSITE PAGE

TOP: The rebirth of the MG sports car began in 1995, with the launch of the MGF. Like the stillborn ADO21 project of 1969/1970, this car featured a mid-mounted transverse engine/gearbox. With a choice of 16-valve/twin cam 118bhp or 143bhp 1.8-litre engines, the MGF was a much faster car than the MGB had ever been.

BOTTOM: The MGF, introduced in 1995, had a totally different profile from the MGB. This was not merely because fashions had moved on in thirty years, but because the MGFs engine and gearbox was mounted transversely behind the seats. Sales went ahead at around 10,000 cars a year – which was all that the tooling could accommodate – and a new-generation car was expected to follow in the early 2000s.

Index

References to Abingdon, BMC, British Leyland, MG, and their related models, are so frequent that these have not been separately indexed.

Alfa Romeo (and models) 7, 16, 33
Aston Martin 90
Austin (and models) 7, 60, 90
Austin-Healey (and models) 5–8, 11, 15, 31, 59–60, 63, 65, 71
Austin-Morris 89
Austin-Rover (and models) 90

Bishop, David 90
BMW 77
British Aerospace 91
British Motor Heritage (BMH) 90–91
British Motor Industry Heritage Trust 90
British Car Auctions 90

Citroën 77
Costello, Ken 73
Curtis, Alan 90

factories:
    Acocks Green (Rover) 76
    Coventry (Morris Bodies Branch) 12, 14, 30–31, 63
    Coventry (Morris Engines Branch) 63
    Cowley 14, 31, 63, 76, 90–91
    Longbridge 14, 31, 51, 89, 90–91
    Swindon (Pressed Steel) 14, 31, 63, 76, 90
    'Tractors & Transmissions' (Birmingham) 14, 63
Fiat (and models) 7, 16, 33, 51
Ford Capri 3000 65, 77

Healey, Donald 59

Jaguar E-Type 61

Land Rover 91
Lotus 90

Mayflower 91
MG Car Club 38

MG models:
    18/80 6
    ADO 21 90, 94
    EX234 89
    Magnette ZA 7–8
    Metro 6R4 92
    MGA 5–8, 11–13, 16
    MGF 91, 94
    Midget 6, 8, 11
    TA/TB/TC 6
    TD/TF 6–7
MG Owners Club 38
Michelotti, Giovanni 16, 30
Morgan 91
Morris (and models) 6

Nissan-Datsun (and models) 7, 65
Nuffield, Lord (formerly William Morris) 5–6
Nuffield Organization 6

Pininfarina 9, 16, 51, 89
Pressed Steel Co. Ltd 7, 14, 28

Range Rover 74–75
Reliant Scimitar GT and GTE 65, 77
Renault (and models) 21
Rover (and models) 73–76, 86–87, 90–92

Sprague, Peter 90
Sunbeam (and models) 7, 16, 33

Thornley, John 7
Towns, William 90
Triumph (and models) 7, 16, 33, 46, 48, 49, 51, 65, 73, 77, 89
TVR 91

University Motors 65

Wickens, David 90
Wolseley 6